# MILLION DOLLAR WOMEN

### The Essential Guide for Female
### Entrepreneurs Who Want to Go Big

## JULIA PIMSLEUR

### SIMON & SCHUSTER

New York   London   Toronto   Sydney   New Delhi

Simon & Schuster
1230 Avenue of the Americas
New York, NY 10020

First Simon & Schuster hardcover edition October 2015

SIMON & SCHUSTER and colophon are registered trademarks of Simon & Schuster, Inc.

For information about special discounts for bulk purchases,
please contact Simon & Schuster Special Sales at 1-866-506-1949
or business@simonandschuster.com.

The Simon & Schuster Speakers Bureau can bring authors to your live event.
For more information or to book an event,
contact the Simon & Schuster Speakers Bureau at
1-866-248-3049 or visit our website at www.simonspeakers.com.

Interior design by Ruth Lee-Mui
Illustrations by Heather Willems/ImageThink

Manufactured in the United States of America

1   3   5   7   9   10   8   6   4   2

Library of Congress Cataloging-in-Publication Data

Pimsleur, Julia.
Million dollar women : the essential guide for female
entrepreneurs who want to go big / Julia Pimsleur.
pages cm
Includes bibliographical references.
1. Women-owned business enterprises. 2. New business enterprises. 3. Fund raising. I. Title.
HD2341.P5197 2015
658.4'09082—dc23
2015011025

ISBN 978-1-4767-9029-9
ISBN 978-1-4767-9032-9 (ebook)

*To My Mother. And All the Women Who Dared.*

# CONTENTS

# INTRODUCTION

## BECOME A MILLION DOLLAR WOMAN

"What are your gross margins?" Jeff asked me. I froze. Jeff and his colleague, venture capitalists (VCs), in button-down shirts and jeans, were asking about my company's financials. Despite their just-out-of-college look, I knew they could write my company a check for millions. Jeff looked at me expectantly.[1]

"That is a good question. I'll have to get back to you on that," I answered with as much confidence as I could feign. I knew what my *margins* were.[2] Were *gross* margins the same thing? Or was that something different? I certainly couldn't ask Jeff. I wasn't sure I had the skills or the swagger to get through this meeting, nor the dozens like it I had coming up. But I knew that if I wanted to get my business funded I had better figure it out, and fast.

Needing money for your business and not knowing how to get it is a situation women are facing in increasing numbers. Over the past twenty years, American women started close to *twice* as many businesses as men,[3] but we still tend to stay small. Only 3 percent of female business owners ever make north of $1 million in revenues, which is considered just getting off "Go" in the business world.[4] By comparison, 6 percent of businesses founded by men make over $1 million in revenues. Most women entrepreneurs are running kitchen-table businesses, just getting by or, worse, running out of cash and shutting down. When my company passed the $1 million mark a few years ago, I got a call from a journalist who wanted to profile me along with other women whose businesses were making "high revenues." I was partly flattered, but I was mainly stunned. *Why are so few women running businesses that make bank?* I decided to find out and to help push that 3 percent number into the double digits. The year after I got that call, I raised $2.1 million in venture capital, exceeded our prior year sales by 85 percent, and on weekends started teaching other women how to raise angel and venture capital in my conference room.

I believe that financial freedom is one of the last front lines of feminism. It's shocking to think that even though we won the vote in 1920, until the Equal Credit Opportunity Act of 1974 we could still be turned away when we tried to buy a house or get a credit card in our own name.[5] We still have a long way to go to achieve financial parity with men, whether it's surpassing 77 cents on the dollar or earning six-figure salaries as CEOs. Today the average revenues of women-owned businesses are still just 27 percent of the average revenues of men-owned businesses.[6]

Recent books written for women who want to excel professionally, like Sheryl Sandberg's *Lean In* and Mika Brzezinski's *Knowing Your Value*, offer road maps for women in corporate America to ascend to the corner office. Now it's time to meet women who, instead of *leaning* in, simply left corporate America (or never entered) and *marched* in to the world of entrepreneurship. They have raised capital, developed powerful networks, and generated multimillion-dollar companies from scratch. We are the Million Dollar Women, and I will show you how to become one of us.

I say "us" because, after meeting with dozens of Jeffs (and very few Janes), I learned the "fundraising dance" and raised $2.1 million in venture capital, which enabled me to turn my small business into one with multimillion-dollar revenues. When I started Little Pim, a company that produces a program for young children to learn a foreign language at home, I wanted to create an exceptional language-learning experience for young children. I knew it could be more than a "lifestyle" business, but I wasn't sure how big I could take it. At one point I hit a wall and even considered shutting down. Instead I doubled down on my dream. I realized that I had to think and behave differently in order to become the CEO of a multimillion-dollar company.

To get my business to start producing different results, I had to change my mindset, get new skills, and raise capital. I had to seek out experts and coaches who could help me tackle my greatest fears and help me evolve from a creative person with a business idea into a CEO running a business with a creative idea at the center of it. *Million Dollar Women* will give you a mirror to look at your own mindset and skills and will help you accelerate the process of taking your business past the million-dollar milestone.

When I was trying to get to $1 million in revenues, I *wished* I could have learned from women who knew what it took. I have worked with incredible advisors, coaches, and mentors—and just about all of them are men. I knew there had to be women out there building big companies, but I rarely read about them in the press and didn't have access to any million dollar women to ask how I could get there too.

Despite all the media hype around entrepreneurship, the only women entrepreneurs most people can name are Oprah Winfrey and Martha Stewart. They may also know of Sara Blakely, whose Spanx undergarment empire made her one of the wealthiest women in America. Then it's usually "Um . . . who else?" I believe the one thing we can *all* do to help women get farther faster is to share our stories so that we can help our entrepreneurial sisters think big—and learn from one another's milestones and mistakes.

In that spirit, I am delighted to introduce you to inspiring women from across America who run successful companies they built from scratch. The entrepreneurs in the sidebars of these pages are not yet featured in *Forbes Most Powerful Women*. These are stories of women who are five or ten years into their journey as successful business owners. They are not that far ahead of you on the hike up the entrepreneurial mountain, and you can learn from their every move. We are at what I like to call Mount Everest Base Camp. A tiny percentage of hikers who set out to climb to the top of Everest, which is at an altitude of 29,000 feet, actually make it. Most never even make it to Base Camp, at 18,000 feet. It is widely documented that 50 percent of all new businesses fail within the first five years. Getting to Base Camp is a huge achievement. It's a staging ground for the determined, where they can share war stories and get ready for the next part of the climb.

Not all of the Million Dollar Women featured in these pages will go on to reach the peak, but they have all built thriving companies—and they've done it, by and large, without attending business school, marrying into money, or benefiting from a trust fund. They will save you many blisters by letting you in on how they made the climb to 18,000 feet and which trails to take. They are running companies in tech, aviation, fashion, education, and e-commerce, creating amazing work cultures, raising children, giving back to their communities, and loving (almost) every minute of it. They are powerful examples of what's possible if you think big. We all got to witness firsthand what is possible for the determined when swimmer Diana Nyad became the first person in the world to swim continuously from Florida to Cuba, at the age of sixty-four, after four previous failed attempts (check out her TED Talk to hear the whole inspiring story). "I'll find a way" is what she said to her team on the day she finally succeeded and swam nearly fifty-three hours to victory.

The past decade has seen an explosion of women starting businesses. In fact, we have started twice as many businesses as men have! We too are trying to "find a way" despite swimming through cold and predator-filled waters. There are over 120 million of us worldwide and close to 10 million here in the United States. We are responsible for $1.4 trillion in revenues every year and have a collective 7.9 million employees in the United States alone.[7] Women are also getting advanced degrees in ever higher numbers and are emerging confident in their abilities. Starting in 2010, for the first time ever, women earned more advanced degrees than men.[8] Around the world, 60 percent of undergraduate students and 30 percent of students at the top business schools are women. Young women used to pursue higher education wanting to be lawyers or doctors; now many want to be founders and CEOs.

You probably know a woman starting or running her own business. She might be a high-energy woman in her thirties who saw her mother fight against glass ceilings and vowed that she would never experience that frustration. She might be a "mompreneur" who wondered why a product she wanted for her child didn't exist and decided to go out and create it. She might be a driven twenty-something who grew up programming code, started her own tech company, and is launching a new app or platform. We are everywhere. Free and low-cost business tools are more readily available than ever before, and emerging entrepreneurs are inspired by wanting to solve problems in new ways and by seeing peers take companies from zero to $100 million in the space of a few years.

And yet I worry. Where will the women who are starting businesses today be in five years? Will they be running the next Dry Bar or Care.com?

Will they be Million Dollar Women? Or will they be filing for bankruptcy, selling their office furniture, and revising their LinkedIn profiles? Close to 97 percent of women who own a business are solo practitioners with no employees. Women are *twice* as likely as men to shut down their business because they run out of money.[9] I want to help more women see that raising capital in order to grow high-revenue-generating businesses is within their reach. Having investors often provides the runway and the right partners to achieve success.

The precarious state of affairs for women entrepreneurs is not the result of women working less hard than men or being less capable. It's largely because most women are still not thinking big enough or going out to raise the dollars that will fuel their business. Women start their businesses with half as much capital as men do, and this trend is not changing fast enough. Recently I was speaking with a woman entrepreneur who has a fashion consulting business. She told me she was having a great year with her company but was also having trouble getting the business to grow beyond what she could take on herself. I asked if she'd considered raising money to hire new staff, scale up, and go after a bigger market. She hadn't, and what's more, she hadn't even realized that having more money could solve nearly every problem she identified. If she had capital, she could hire additional staff, invest more in marketing, focus on the parts of her business that are the most profitable, and work on the big-picture plan.

I have had dozens of conversations like this. Women entrepreneurs often don't pursue the capital they need to properly execute a big vision. While raising money is tough for any entrepreneur, regardless of gender, it's exponentially harder for women. Less than 12 percent of all growth capital in the United States, and less than 7 percent of high-dollar venture capital, is invested in women-run businesses.[10]

Men tend to raise more money than we do, take more risks, network more aggressively, and own more of the high-revenue-generating businesses. So how can we learn to do this, and do it our way? If you follow the steps I outline here and read my interviews with top business and investment industry insiders, you will be giant strides closer to becoming one of the Million Dollar Women you'll meet in these pages. If you want to go deeper into one of the topics, such as how to determine if you have a "fundable" business or more of a "lifestyle" business, how to raise money, or how to break through limiting beliefs you may have about yourself as a CEO, head over to juliapimsleur.com. You'll find free resources, online courses, and tools to help you get to the next level—faster. I truly believe you can get there on your own, but I can help you get there faster, and with fewer fires to put out along the way!

## THE TRIPLE WIN

I am passionate about helping more women build multimillion-dollar businesses because it gives us access to what I call "the Triple Win": Money, Meaning, and Mobility.

Men traditionally gauge "success" by the number of zeros at the end of their annual revenues or what they sold their companies for. As women, we want the big financial win, but not just that. We know *Money* gives us the ability to make decisions about where we live, where our kids go to school, and whom we marry (or whether to marry). As women entrepreneurs, we also want to do work that has *Meaning* and that provides solutions to problems we have grappled with in our own lives. We want the work that absorbs so much of our time and energy to count for something beyond just a paycheck, especially when it takes us away from our children and family. We want to run a business that puts our talents to the best and highest use.

Last but not least—and sometimes it comes first in our priorities—is *Mobility*. As entrepreneurs we are willing to work twenty-three of twenty-four hours each day, but we want to choose which twenty-three and from where! Our work is what gives us the mobility and flexibility to stay home with a sick child, to travel, to see our kids' school plays, to work remotely, or to serve on nonprofit boards. As a CEO I cherish having the freedom to work how, when, and where I want. Yes, every so often I envy my friends who work for large companies when I see them able to leave their work at the office. But I also know that the corporate jobs that look secure really aren't. Workers today can expect to change jobs fifteen to twenty times in the course of their lives.[11] Those "safe" corporate positions are less secure than ever. In the 2008 recession, 19 percent of senior-level women lost their jobs, compared to 6 percent of senior-level men.[12]

As Million Dollar Women we can model this Triple Win and create a new definition of success. We can show our children that it's possible to work hard at something we love, to excel at it, and to still be a mom, friend, spouse, or auntie. We can run our board meetings, fly to China to visit our manufacturers, sell our products on TV, train for a marathon, get to curriculum night at school, and create an office culture that doesn't penalize workers for taking maternity leave.

Some women say they don't want to "go big" because it will come with too many responsibilities outside the home, like overseeing a staff and managing outside investors. At first, it may seem overwhelming. But Million Dollar Women know that running a high-earning company means having a senior-level team who handle most of the day-to-day operations and who help you successfully implement your vision. This gives you more time to work on the parts of the business you love, become a better manager and cultivator of talent for your staff, and, ultimately, gain more freedom in every respect.

Here's some good news: you do not need a business or finance background to put the lessons in this book to work right away. I did not go to business school, and neither did most of the women interviewed in this book. The Triple Win requires that you master just two things: the right mindset and the right skill set. It's that simple, but it's not easy. I am here to show you the difference between running a business that works and running a business that works for you.

I want you to get to $1 million, and then wave at it in the rearview mirror as you cruise to $5 million, $10 million, and beyond. It may require raising capital, even though that could be the furthest thing from your mind today. It may require changing how you structure your work and personal life. Even if you're not striving to reach a certain dollar milestone in revenues, you can work more efficiently and effectively in whatever size business you have. The time you'll free up will be yours to read novels, learn Spanish, play with your kids, binge-watch your favorite series—or go change the world.

The exercises at the end of this book—which you can complete here or download at juliapimsleur.com—will help you customize the teachings for your business and put them to work right away. This book is for women who want to run a business that makes *at least* $1 million, women founders considering fundraising, solo practitioner consultants who want to up their game, or young women curious about the entrepreneurial life. I've included a glossary too in case you get stuck on any terms.

Ten key Million Dollar Women mantras are represented throughout this book in illustrated form as cuff bracelets—these are like virtual bracelets you can wear whenever you need an extra boost. Why cuffs? Because when I was workshopping this book with some of my most cherished entrepreneurial sisters—the Million Dollar Women Brain Trust—I learned that we all have personal mantras we rely on to keep forging ahead. All of us described these mantras as instruments of self-protection, like the bullet-proof cuffs worn by Wonder Woman. When I was raising money for my company, I would mentally run through mantras to shore myself up, especially before going in front of rooms packed with men in suits who were my potential investors. These mantras included "If it were easy, everyone would do it" and "Have the fear. Do it anyway."

Wonder Woman cuffs may seem goofy, but all of us in the Brain Trust sort of adore this kitsch symbol of power. In Wonder Woman folklore, it was her mother, the Queen of the Amazons, who gave her the bracelets, made from the shield of the Greek goddess of wisdom and strategy, Athena. The cuffs made Wonder Woman indestructible. She could even slam them together to create a force wave that repelled her greatest adversaries, a neat trick that Million Dollar Women have borrowed, especially in venture capital negotiations!

I hope that when you go to pitch for funding in rooms full of "suits" (and by the time you read this, I hope that more of those suits will be worn by women), you will virtually slip on your favorite cuffs and let them unleash your entrepreneurial superpowers. Your Million Dollar Women sisters have been in those rooms, and we are right there with you. Once you're done with the book, go to juliapimsleur.com to share your own mantras with me and other women entrepreneurs. My goal in writing this book is to help one million women get to the one million in revenues mark. Whether you are currently making $50,000 a year or $500,000, have a business you just launched or are contemplating your first fundraising round, you are already on your way. It's time to get your gear together for the thrilling and will-testing climb ahead.

One of the cuffs I turn to the most when I'm feeling daunted is: "Fortune favors the brave." (*Fortes fortuna juvat.*) When you summon your courage and decide to do what you have never done before, amazing things can happen. So let's get brave, and let's get started.

# 1

## HOW I GOT OFF THE ENTREPRENEUR'S HAMSTER WHEEL

To be successful at running a small business, we need to work hard and keep driving forward. And yet positive traits like perseverance and diligence may turn us into little hamsters, turning the wheel with increasing speed but not getting anywhere. This attitude of "I'll just work harder" is a very female approach to getting ahead and may be the very thing that prevents us from taking our businesses big.

I myself was on that wheel for four years, running as fast as I could as a small business owner. Until things started falling apart, I didn't even stop to ask whether that exertion was taking me where I wanted to go. The wake-up call came when one of my advisors told me, "You can be *low* on cash for a long time, but you can only *run out* of cash once." I had bills that were starting to exceed the incoming checks, and we hadn't found a way to turbocharge our sales.

In the end, I managed to avoid running out of money, and I ultimately went on to raise capital and build a multimillion-dollar company. But before I explain how all that happened, I need to rewind a bit. My entrepreneurial story actually starts way back, in a time that most of us would prefer to forget: middle school.

## DIAPERING FOR DOLLARS

On the first day of my summer vacation at the end of eighth grade, I rode in the backseat of an Audi with two little boys to the Hamptons, where many well-to-do New York families spend summer vacations.

I was to be a mother's helper, working for an exasperated Manhattan mom, Marilyn. She was happy just to have help, any help, with her rowdy three- and five-year-old boys, even from a fourteen-year-old girl with little actual experience.

The job entailed living in their unfinished basement and spending endless hours on the floor crashing Matchbox cars while making explosion sound effects. I was at the beck and call of frazzled Marilyn and weathered verbal abuse from her husband, a disgruntled day-trading dad who joined us on weekends. This job wore perilously thin after about two weeks.

On the beach I met up with other indentured servants like myself, teenage girls doing one of the only money-making jobs available to us: diapering for dollars. After the first month, three of the girls had quit, preferring to go back to Manhattan and dodge cockroaches and piles of smelly garbage in the city streets rather than suffer one more day of little Michael's fits when his chicken wasn't cut up the right way.

By August it was down to just one other mother's helper and me, commiserating on beaches over sand-laced French fries. I did feel quite grown up, having two young children in my charge, and I did have my first make-out session on a waterbed, but overall I was pretty miserable. I remember when my last remaining mother's helper friend decided to bail. I wanted so much to follow her! Even though the boys insisted on playing the soundtrack from *Annie* on a twenty-four-hour loop and the day-trading dad said inappropriate things to me like "You will probably be fat by the time you are eighteen," I still stayed. I simply didn't want to be a quitter.

On my last day Marilyn came down to the basement and handed me a $100 tip. On top of the $85 per week I had made, I had cleared nearly $1,000. It was a heady feeling for a girl of fourteen, and I was hooked right then on financial freedom. I went back to the Hamptons the following two summers and racked up several thousand dollars, which I saved to spend in part on a four-week trip to Italy with my best friend at age seventeen. I managed to pick better and better families each time I went back to the Hamptons, and those summers turned out to be a terrific first business school. On those beaches I learned some of the most important skills I needed to set me up for my career: hard work, patience, and keeping the clients happy.

I had also stumbled on one of the most important ingredients of entrepreneurship, the one that would later allow me to create a company, narrowly avoid bankruptcy, and fire people who had to go: *grit*. Without grit, of which a key part is resilience, no one has any business going into business. As any entrepreneur will tell you, whatever can go wrong *will*—and usually within the first year. Those who have grit keep on going and, like water around rocks, find a new way forward. Those who don't pack up and go back to their cubicle.

Grit got me pretty far in life. I had always prided myself on being a hard worker who cruised down long task lists. Even as a young mother with two kids, I was the one who created the class contact list and ran the parent book club. I loved to think I was the walking example of "Ask a busy person if you want to get something done."

But over time I realized that grit had also become a liability. I was so good at hunkering down and getting the job done, so focused on taking care of others, that I couldn't see the bigger picture. Grit wasn't going to give me the confidence to take the greater risks I needed to take to scale up my business. Grit wasn't going to convince institutional investors to bet on me. How could I take my $150,000-per-year company and turn it into a $1.5-million and eventually a $15-million-per-year company? Not by buckling down and working eighty hours instead of sixty. I realized I needed to change *how* I was working, not just *how much*.

One of my coaches, Gina Mollicone-Long, likes to invoke an old proverb about change: "You can't cross a twenty-foot chasm in two ten-foot leaps." Sometimes you have to come up with a totally new plan to catapult yourself to the other side—or risk falling into the abyss after your first big leap.

## THE BIRTH OF LITTLE PIM

Fast-forward twenty-something years from middle school. When my first son, Emmett, was born, teaching him French was high on my priorities list. I was raised bilingual in French and English, and this led to what I considered some of my most valuable experiences: scholarships to top schools, the confidence that comes from being effortlessly good at something, living and working in France, and jobs in international film production. I was determined to give Emmett these same advantages in life. Besides, language education runs in our family. My father, Dr. Paul Pimsleur, created a language-learning method that's still widely used today. He passed away when I was eight, but has left behind a legacy I have always been extremely proud of: the Pimsleur Method. I love meeting people all over the world who have used Pimsleur to become conversational in French, Spanish, or Chinese and can say "Will you have a drink with me at seven o'clock?" in multiple Pimsleur languages!

I was lucky that I became fluent in French at age six and don't even remember learning. We were living in Paris for my father's work, and I attended a French public school. My brother and I became bilingual in a matter of three months, and this has paid off over my entire lifetime. How was I going to give this gift to my son Emmett here in the United States? I sang him traditional French lullabies like "Frère Jacques" and spoke to him in French whenever we played, but I knew it would require far more exposure for him to grasp the language. My husband didn't speak French, and we had plans to hire a full-time sitter when I went back to work. She was great with babies, but she didn't speak French either.

As I watched Emmett's fascination with anything involving a screen, whether it was my phone, *Sesame Street*, or made-for-children DVDs, it dawned on me: Would he know the difference if I put on a French video instead? I wanted to start exposing him to the sounds and accents of the French language but still keep him entertained. I searched the Internet and bookstores for language-teaching materials and found a French DVD made for babies, which I played for him. It had low production values, and even worse, was riddled with translation mistakes.

Still on maternity leave, I had some time on my hands and started researching the impact of learning a second language at an early age. I knew intuitively and from my own experience that young was the best time to learn, but was still surprised when I started finding study after study showing that zero-to-six is a critical window during which we can learn up to three languages with ease. After age six there is a steep drop-off in our ability to learn a second language, and another after age ten. And meanwhile, try as I might, I could not find a language DVD for Emmett that I didn't want to fling across the room after five minutes.

In the made-for-TV version of my story, I would then have gone out and raised $3 million, created an award-winning series, opened offices with a staff of ten, and grown the company to $15 million in revenues within two years.

What really happened was this: while breast-feeding, going back to my full-time job, and being semi-delirious from lack of sleep, I couldn't get the idea out of my head that *someone* should create a better way for kids to learn languages. It should be a video series specifically designed for young children, with a toddler-friendly character and rich content. *Someone* who cared about languages. *Someone* who could make high-quality videos. It took a full three months to realize that *someone* was me.

I had been a documentary filmmaker. I loved languages and spoke several and came from the Pimsleur family, considered language-teaching "royalty" in some circles. Plus, I was a mom. But I was making a significant portion of our family's income at that time, and my husband, Darren, had just started a demanding new job. How would my starting a business affect our finances and our relationship? Besides, I hadn't gone to business school. Not to mention, I had a baby at home and didn't want to detract from being the best mother I could be. And—oh, right—I didn't have the cash.

But as any entrepreneur will tell you, sometimes an idea takes on a life of its own; it keeps coming around like a stray cat for food until you take it in permanently. I talked to my family about the idea for a language-teaching DVD series, and my husband and mother both agreed that it sounded like a great business opportunity. Darren suggested I create language schools for young children, but that was far less appealing to me. I didn't like the idea of managing dozens and ultimately hundreds of people or having to deal with finding locations and getting permits to hold classes. Plus, the DVD series called on my background as a filmmaker and felt like something I could start on the side, without quitting my job. I also knew instinctively what I didn't yet have the business words for: that the media company was more *scalable* than the schools company. The margins were higher, and making DVDs would be a onetime *sunk cost* that could then be recouped over time.

My mother came up with the idea that the main teacher of the series should be a panda bear, which seemed like a toddler-friendly and original choice. We liked the idea of a panda in part because babies see black and white better than color, and panda bears come from China, introducing children to the idea of another country. I found an undiscovered illustrator online who created a rotund and delightfully mischievous-looking panda for a nominal fee. We named the character "Little Pim" and our little language teacher was born.

Bit by bit I moved on to other parts of the business: my lawyer friend Dominique Bravo helped me draw up contracts with the illustrator and file for a copyright. A neuroscientist friend of the family, Dr. April Benasich, who is well known for her research on how babies and toddlers learn languages, signed on as an advisor. I recruited two bright Columbia Business School students to help me flesh out a business plan. We began meeting every other Saturday for an hour and a half (they worked for yogurt parfaits at Le Pain Quotidien bakery), and they helped me map out how Little Pim could become a viable business. They used exclusive business databases at Columbia to research the trajectory of successful DVD companies and to find stats on the educational video market.

Still, I did not quit my job or even consider it. My husband was earning a decent salary, but not enough to support all three of us or fund a new business. We had nominal savings. Furthermore I loved my job as a nonprofit fundraiser, working with Echoing Green, an organization that granted fellowships to social change makers. I had good benefits, smart colleagues, meaningful work, and manageable hours. But I couldn't get Little Pim out of my head. When Emmett was napping or if I couldn't fall back asleep after an early-morning breast-feeding, I would sketch storyboards of Little Pim the panda and his adventures and pore over children's books with titles like *First Thousand Words in French*.

The business research the Columbia grad students did suggested that there was a large and expanding market for kids' educational videos. The family DVD market alone was $5.3 billion, and language learning worldwide was $85 billion. Rosetta Stone, the market leader in the United States, was making over $250 million per year. But it was harder to estimate how many parents cared about foreign-language learning for kids. I was passionate about it, and I knew other parents in New York and other major cities who felt the same way, but what about parents across the United States? And around the world? We realized we were likely going after a niche market of parents who cared, but I was convinced there was a broader interest in foreign-language teaching for kids that had not yet been tapped. Capitalizing on the Pimsleur brand, with a cute panda teacher and high-quality videos, I felt we could drive demand and expand the market for early-language learning beyond what it had been. I was also passionate about what I saw as "democratizing" early-language learning—why should this incredible benefit be available only to kids of the 1 percent whose parents could afford a foreign-born nanny or expensive language classes? Little Pim would be sold for the same price as other children's videos and make language learning possible for millions of young children.

I decided to take the Little Pim idea to the publishing company that had bought the rights to the Pimsleur Method from our family some ten years earlier. It made perfect sense to me that a publisher would want to expand its language empire into selling a product for little kids, and I went to my first meeting full of optimism. The Pimsleur Method had become one of the best-selling methods for adults. My mother still received royalties, but otherwise we were no longer involved in the business. I was welcomed by the publishing executives, and that meeting led to more meetings. But six months later I had been through four rounds of meetings and had not yet gotten a real yes or no.

## FORGET ABOUT THE BIG BOYS

In the midst of the hurry-up-and-wait meetings with the publishing company that winter and spring, Darren and I decided to go to Vietnam for ten days, our first big trip since we had become parents. We left two-year-old Emmett with Darren's parents in California and set off for Hanoi, the capital. In Vietnam there was widespread poverty; everyone seemed to be working so hard yet earning so little. As we traveled through the lush green countryside crisscrossed with rice fields, I thought about the lives of the young mothers I saw. Entire families were huddled around buckets of water, bathing and cooking. I felt deeply humbled when I thought about my own life and dreams for my son and realized that the greatest hope a young mother had for her son here was that he work in Hanoi as a waiter and escape the $1-per-day wages of the rice fields.

As we traveled south to the coastal town of Hoi An, I began to think seriously about the privileges I had back home (a job, a supportive family, degrees from prestigious institutions) and suddenly felt I had no excuse for not trying to create this new business. So what if the publishing company didn't want to partner with me? So what if I hadn't gone to business school? What was the worst thing that could happen? If it didn't work out, I could always go back to fundraising for nonprofits.

I also thought about my great-grandmother Ada Goldwater, a Russian Jewish immigrant who had opened a cigarette and candy shop on lower Broadway in New York in the early 1900s. Her husband died at thirty-six of appendicitis, leaving her with six young children. Thanks to that shop, she provided for her children all through the Depression and beyond. Her daughter Meira, my maternal grandmother, went on to have an important career in the days when women rarely got past secretary; she was the chief of acquisitions for the law library at Columbia University for fifty years. Meira's sister, my amazing great-aunt Beatie, who was four feet, ten inches tall and wore signature cat's-eye glasses, used to always remind me that I come from a long line of enterprising women. "Just remember," she'd say in her heavy New York accent, "Goldwater girls are smart!"

I finally realized I shouldn't wait for the big boys in publishing to decide my fate. If Little Pim was going to happen, it was up to me, and me alone, to move ahead. To borrow one of my own metaphors from my nonprofit fundraising days: people like to board a train that is leaving the station. The Little Pim train needed to blow the whistle and get moving.

## OUR FIRST OUTSIDE INVESTORS

I decided to produce a pilot of what a Little Pim video would look like, convinced that if people could see what I saw in my head, they would understand its potential to teach and entertain. Through contacts in the film and video world from my film-producing days, I found a freelance producer to manage the project for a small fee. My mother, who had once had her own small documentary company, volunteered to help. We put together a crew, recruited mothers and their kids to be in the pilot, and filmed in Emmett's preschool and in my lawyer and friend Dominique's

playroom in Brooklyn. Working with the kids was challenging but also really fun, and we captured some adorable moments. We came away with hours of footage and couldn't wait to get into the editing room.

I also formally incorporated Little Pim. I invested $10,000 and another $15,000 borrowed from my mother. I opened a Little Pim Corporation bank account and got an EIN number, and suddenly it all felt very official.

But we were running through our production money fast and editing took longer than expected, eating up cash to pay the editor. So I asked my close friends Mark and Jason to put in $20,000 as a loan that would convert into stock. They said yes and that infusion of capital really saved the day. With these funds we were able to add one more week of editing, commission music, and get to the end of the pilot production.

Once I had a pilot, things started to fall into place. I showed it over coffee to Rebecca, a friend from college. I had planned to ask her for advice or a small investment and was overjoyed when, after watching the five-minute video, she said, "This is a gold mine! I want to invest." A few months later Rebecca invested $100,000 through her family's trust, the first significant money I raised from friends and family.

Rebecca's reaction helped give me the confidence to approach other people in my extended circle. My first big angel investment came from an unlikely source, via my mother's yoga retreat buddy. Her friend's daughter-in-law, Marion, had a four-year-old daughter who had learned sign language from a video series when she was a toddler. As a result Marion was a big believer in educational videos as teaching tools. She and her husband were well off, but Marion was no average wife of a man of means. She had worked as a professional investor and had graduated from a top business school. She wanted not only to invest but to help run the company, drawing on her business acumen and her connections in early education. It was time to get a start-up lawyer. Dominique introduced me to her friend Jonathan, who was willing to give me a favorable rate and had worked with many new companies raising capital. He helped me assess my options for taking in this first investment, understand all the legal terms I needed to know, and "paper" the deal with convertible notes (see glossary).

Marion and her husband and mother-in-law teamed up and invested more than $200,000. They negotiated a deal whereby they would own close to 30 percent of the company and invested through a convertible loan that would turn into stock when we raised our first official round of financing. It was a lot of equity for me to hand over, but it also meant that I could take the train even farther out of the station. I was eager to produce more videos and set up our website rather than spend many more months fundraising. I agonized over it a bit, but I took the deal.

Now that I had a lead funder, we could set the valuation of the company. The "valuation" is what the investor is willing to accept as the company's worth. With Marion on board, we set the valuation at $3 million. I came up with this number by talking to advisors, my Columbia business students, and my lawyer. Even though we didn't have a product yet, we knew the Pimsleur name had value and felt that we could also base the company's potential earnings on the Baby Einstein success story (those DVDs were produced by a mom in her basement, who then went from $1M to $25M in revenues in five years and sold her company to Disney).

Jonathan advised me that while I might be able to find an investor who didn't ask for as much equity as Marion did, having her investment in place would attract other investors. When I recently asked him whether he still thought that was the right decision, he replied, "Was your original deal with her a good deal? Yes, it was, because you gained a motivated, aggressive champion, and you gained credibility by having raised angel money."

Jonathan was right that money attracts money. When I went out to raise capital a few months later, we had a lead investor, we had a national distribution deal with Barnes & Noble in the works, and we had revenues. Over the ensuing months I steered conversations with friends and family about Little Pim into conversations about capital and how they could help. I raised money in $10,000 and $20,000 increments until I had over $400,000, the amount I needed to produce the first three DVDs and launch our website. My background as a fundraiser really came in handy, as I felt relatively comfortable having conversations about money and pitching to potential investors. This was the first time I was asking for investments instead of donations, but the skills were transferable.

The people who did become investors included the parents of one of my son's friends from the playground (both parents worked at major banks), a dear old family friend and his partner who had a family trust, a friend who was legal counsel for a large media company, and the brother-in-law of my friend Rebecca.

In addition to these precious yeses, I pitched to dozens of people who said no for a variety of reasons: they didn't have enough disposable income, didn't understand the kids' video market well enough, or didn't want to get involved in an early-stage company. I never took offense or made it uncomfortable for them if they said no. In some cases I found other ways to involve them, like asking them to bring their children to a film shoot or loan us their home for filming. As a former filmmaker, I had asked people for these kinds of favors before. I had seen that, far from being irked that I was asking for a favor, people generally enjoyed taking part in a creative endeavor, even if it meant having fifty toddlers and moms traipse in and out of their basement for a film shoot.

Some of the parents who invested had children who were featured in our pilot, so they felt tied to our project. That personal connection definitely helped to seal the deal. I had everyone sign a simple subscription agreement, which gave them a certain number of common stock shares in exchange for their investment.

Part of what gave me confidence to ask so many friends—and friends of friends—for money is that I truly felt, *If I see such a big opportunity with Little Pim that I am willing to give up a lucrative career and work like mad to bring this to life, why wouldn't I give my friends a chance to be part of it?* I also took comfort in what my lawyer explained were the regulations about "accredited investors." Everyone who invested would have to qualify as an accredited investor, which the Securities and Exchange Commission defines as an individual or couple with over $1 million in net worth or who earn over $200,000 in income per year for three consecutive years. In other words, friends who invested couldn't be risking their nest eggs. The money they invested in Little Pim was part of their investment portfolio. If it wasn't put to work growing my company, it would sit in their bank account or get invested in someone else's company.

I did fear that if I took their investments and the company didn't become the über-success I thought it would be, it could damage these friendships. But I also knew I would work tirelessly to see that my friends' investments doubled, tripled, or more when the company sold. I was still the one with the most to gain or lose, and had every motivation to make this a big win.

I was also spending the money while I was raising it. I was still working full-time but visited the editing room as often as I could after hours to check in with my producers and approve final cuts of the three videos we were producing in Spanish, French, and Chinese. We hired two language advisors for each of the languages and spent hours poring over scripts and translations, making sure we had every accent and nuance correct. Dr. Benasich, my neuroscientist advisor, helped us ensure the method was effective and age-appropriate. Thank goodness I had free labor in my mother, who had worked closely with my father on the Pimsleur Method, and at home I had a very involved husband and a loving babysitter whom my son adored.

By November 2007 we were ready to go live with our first three language-teaching videos, which we could sell individually or as a bundled set. We also added a plush Little Pim panda so kids could hold Little Pim and the sets would seem more "giftable." The website was functional, if not very sophisticated. We had a warehouse in California ready to take orders and ship the product.

I was feeling great about making our first few hundred sales, and had growing confidence in my entrepreneurial abilities. It was fantastic to see everything coming together, though I was pulled in what felt like six different directions between my full-time job, my baby, going to my husband's work functions, and managing Little Pim by email at all times of the day and night. I knew I couldn't go on like this very long. It required keeping too many balls in the air and getting too little sleep or downtime. I hoped the DVDs would sell well that first holiday season and that soon I could work at Little Pim full time.

In one particularly high high and low low, we found out we were going to be featured on the *Today* show in December! That would really boost our brand. We expected it would drive hundreds, maybe even thousands of sales. My lead investor, Marion, insisted we spend $80,000 on making additional DVDs so that when the piece aired, we would have enough to fill orders. But as so often happens in television, the story was postponed indefinitely, and we were stuck with the $80,000 bill. Thankfully the DVDs weren't perishable and we could sell them over the upcoming year. Even without *Today* (which I did get on eventually) and with no real marketing dollars spent, we made over $55,000 that holiday season. Little Pim was starting to feel like a real business.

## AND STILL THE DAY JOB

Throughout those first months, I continued working full-time fundraising at Echoing Green. Then, just as Little Pim was getting going, I was asked to run the development department of a larger nonprofit. I was torn. I had growing confidence in my fledgling business but didn't feel ready to join Little Pim full-time and give up that direct deposit into my bank account. We'd already completed the production of the first Little Pim series, had a successful initial "friends and family" fundraising round, and sold thousands of units. But I also knew that Little Pim wasn't yet going to pay my bills. The new fundraising job offered a substantial pay increase and better benefits. Also, for the first time in my career, I felt I could ask for exactly the package I wanted and get it.

I forwarded a list of requests to Saul, my potential new employer: a $20,000 raise, non-negotiable 10 a.m. to 6 p.m. hours on days there wasn't an event, a ban on travel beyond the East Coast, Fridays working from home, and a budget to hire new support staff. I also told him that I was starting a business on the side and likely wouldn't stay more than two years.

Saul wasn't put off by my requests and, to my relief, was actually grateful for my honesty about my plans. He was focused on his own immediate goal of pleasing an impatient board that wanted a seasoned development director. As long as I could promise him at least a year, he said, he would agree to all my terms. We shook on it.

The next twelve months involved creating the nonprofit's first major fundraising program, checking on Little Pim every free moment, and still trying to be an attentive mother and wife. I can't say that I succeeded in doing all those things well. But I did build a successful development department at the nonprofit and made my boss look like gold. I loved the time I spent with Emmett and Darren, and I did my best to save my weekends for the family.

I kept pushing Little Pim forward, though I increasingly wondered,

*Toward what?* I felt sure that Little Pim was my future but couldn't yet see how it was going to make enough money to pay me a salary anything close to what I was making as a fundraiser. I also knew that this insane life of two jobs and a baby was not something I could pull off for much longer.

My husband was supportive, but also human. When we met, Darren was still in graduate school and I was already working, and he was four years younger to boot. We didn't have a totally traditional husband-wife model as I was in a way more career-focused than him. I knew he was proud of me and he told friends and family about Little Pim, and yet he was starting to show signs of wear over the long hours I spent on my computer. I was trying to increase our sales of the DVDs by improving the website, doing cross-marketing with other baby-focused companies, and applying for awards. All that took time.

By the time Emmett was two, Little Pim had completed its first year of sales, which had brought in $126,000. We had just one full-time employee, Stacey, a bright young woman I'd found on Craigslist who wore eccentric headbands and wanted to be a writer. She was overqualified to do the administrative tasks I needed, but the job fit with her writing schedule and we liked each other. Stacey sat at a small desk wedged between two documentary film producers in a loft-style office on West 14th Street and oversaw the DVDs being shipped to the warehouse and then to customers. If anything went wrong along that chain, her job was to get it fixed. Marion still helped oversee the business from her home in Connecticut. And I checked in daily at lunch and after work. It was an exciting time, but it was also starting to be untenable. Something had to give.

## RAISING MY FIRST MILLION

Darren and I were thinking of having a second baby, and the job at the nonprofit was losing its appeal as I became more excited about Little Pim's prospects. I stayed up late one night making an Excel spreadsheet of exactly what I thought I would need to launch Little Pim properly: paying myself a salary, making the next set of three DVDs so that there would be six in the series, and paying for online marketing so we could sell more. It came out to about a million dollars in expenses.

I decided it was time to get advice from someone who understood the business world far better than I did. I called up John, the father of my best friend from high school. He had always been a mentor to me, in addition to a kind of second dad, and gave me my first office job at his company when I was in high school. John was a self-made man who came from humble beginnings. I suspected part of our bond was that he saw some of himself in me; I was trying to invent a different future for myself and starting pretty much from scratch, as he had.

John ran a successful hedge fund and was married to one of Little Pim's advisors, so he had been following our progress from the beginning. Over lunch I told him about my passion for Little Pim and the traction we were getting. He shared that he was "awful at languages" and had always regretted that he hadn't learned French. Once an Olympic fencer, he had traveled all over the world, and one of his dearest friends had been a French fencer. He loved that I was making it easier for kids to learn a language. He also saw the company's potential as a business. Then I mustered my courage and told him my dilemma: I thought Little Pim had a real future, a big future, but I couldn't properly run it while staying in my full-time job. I wanted to know where I could get the capital, and could he point me in the right direction?

I thought John might tell me about loans or government programs, but instead he looked me squarely in the eyes and said, "How much do you need?" I said, "About a million." Since I had the budget with me, I pulled it out and ran him through it line by line. He asked questions about the market and our distribution plans, and then said calmly and simply, "I can help you get a million dollars."

That is still one of the most memorable moments of my life. In those eight words John opened up a world of possibility and Little Pim became a real company. Six months later I had left my job and was working full-time at Little Pim. I was also pregnant with our second child.

## CUTTING BACK TO GO FORWARD

I had grown up largely with a single mom on a no-frills budget, so living frugally didn't scare me. Getting ready to go full-time at Little Pim, I made a budget of our home expenses and came up with the bare minimum salary I needed to take from the company. Darren is a minimalist at heart who still fondly remembers calling a VW bus home for six months in his twenties. He didn't mind the cutbacks and was fully supportive of my plan to go full-time. I gave myself a salary that was $30,000 less than I was making as a fundraiser. The $1 million from John hadn't come in the form of a single check, as I'd imagined it would. Instead he took me to meet clients and friends of his and let me pitch, dozens of times, until we had raised over $500,000. The valuation of $3 million stuck, in part because I now had Marion and John helping me defend that number. I got many nos but also enough yeses to fill the coffers halfway. The rest of the $1 million came trickling in over a period of ten months.

During that first year of working full-time on the business, I was always fundraising. I made myself available to meet whenever John had someone interested or if I connected with a friend of a friend who did angel investing through my own networks. I would show up with a short presentation about Little Pim and walk them through my plans. I made sure to emphasize my background in the language business through my father and the set of skills that made me uniquely right for this business (filmmaker/teacher/mother). I talked about the revenues that Baby Einstein and Rosetta Stone generated, and how if we captured even just one-tenth of their earnings, we could be a $25 million company. Each investor had his or her own set of questions and suggestions. It was important to stay flexible and be ready to tell the story a little differently depending on the person in front of me.

For instance, for Arthur, a man in his sixties John introduced me to, who lived in Paris part of the year, I emphasized the benefits of making more kids bilingual. For an investor who saw Little Pim as a business opportunity but didn't have any personal connection to the mission or subject matter, I made sure to give more details about our plans in each sales channel and what the ROI (return on investment) would likely be.

I told people they could expect a 5-times to 10-times return (which meant that when we sold the company they would make five or ten times what they put into it) and that we planned to build up the company to sizable revenues over the upcoming years before selling, unless an opportunity came along sooner. At first all this language felt forced, but John and

Marion helped me with it, and after the first few meetings I relaxed a bit. People always seemed to ask the same types of questions, and soon I knew the answers.

The nos I got this time were largely for the same reasons as the last time: people wanted to invest in something with a faster return, didn't know the children's media space well enough to make an informed decision, or didn't care enough about the field to invest in it. Most of the investors who said yes felt some personal connection to our company's mission of making language learning accessible to young children.

It was during this time of constant pitching that I was introduced to Steve, a friend's husband. He had just sold his business and was looking for investment opportunities. Over lunch at a restaurant near our office on West 14th Street, he decided to put in $200,000 and become one of our first board members. This was a huge win. Steve was an experienced entrepreneur who had built and sold his own software business, and he came with deep business-building and financial experience, two skills I lacked. He was also a great supporter and helped me through the dark days when we needed to negotiate our way out of unfavorable contracts, threaten accounts that wouldn't pay, and put together complicated financials for new investors. My lawyer helped me structure our first official board, made up of Marion, Steve, John, and me.

Meanwhile I was still making ample use of the most talented free labor around: my wonderful mother, Beverly. She helped me choose which words to teach as part of the Little Pim core vocabulary, and she sat with the editor for hours on end while he pulled together all the elements for each of our new language videos. We were working on our second set of videos, as parents were delighted with Volume 1 and were now asking for Volume 2. We were making videos as fast as we could and already had back orders.

In February 2008 my second son, Adrian, was born in the middle of a beautiful snowstorm. My mother was in the Little Pim editing room a few blocks away, working on DVDs 4, 5, and 6, when I called her in labor. "Do you want me in the edit room or the delivery room?" she asked with mock seriousness. I told her to keep editing until she heard from Darren. After many hours of labor and a second C-section, my adorable baby boy came into the world. My mother pulled herself away from editing to be the first one to meet him after Darren and me. Those few days in the hospital were among the happiest in my life. I spent them watching the snow-covered city from my window and cradling little Adrian. I experienced an exquisite and rare period of calm and pure joy. Adrian was born on February 12. Two days later Darren and I shared Valentine's Day hamburgers from a local diner in my hospital room and then took Adrian home.

Life was really good. I felt so fortunate to have that time with my family. Adrian had a delightfully easy personality, and, unlike when Emmett was born and I had to figure everything out on my own (often wishing for CliffsNotes!), our full-time sitter shared looking after the baby. I took three weeks off and then worked part-time from home for another few weeks, managing the business remotely and going into the office around my son's feeding schedule. I stayed in constant touch with my board members to reassure them that business was still moving forward despite my working from home. They were all very supportive—except, ironically, Marion, the only woman on the board. She told me outright that she was not pleased at all that I had a second child right at the time we were trying to push the business forward. During a tense phone conversation she said she was "very disappointed." At one point she blurted, "If you were really serious about Little Pim, you would not have had a second child right now!" I was shocked, then irritated, and finally mad. My children were non-negotiable, and besides, they were a big part of what motivated me to make the business successful.

Our relationship never recovered from that conversation, though Marion stayed on the board for five more years. I also became determined to prove her wrong. I believed I could be a good mother and a successful business owner. Though it was tempting to stay angry at her, I ultimately realized her years working in the male-dominated finance world probably had a lot to do with her comments about my family.

Whenever I had these kinds of conflicts or got to feeling low about how hard it was to run a start-up business, I reminded myself that lots of people would love to run their own company. The reason so few did is that it is bloody hard! To keep moving forward I came up with one of my favorite mantras, and it still is the one I pull out on the bad days:

## WHITEWATER RAFTING THROUGH THE RECESSION

The Spanish, French, and Chinese Volume 2 videos were selling well, and we had more than two hundred accounts at specialty stores across the country, a national distribution deal with Barnes & Noble, and a promising new relationship with PBS Kids Play. Then, in September 2008, the economy crashed. Everything turned upside down, and all nonessential consumer spending ground to a halt. It felt like Armageddon, especially because Darren and I lived next to the Financial District, headquarters of Goldman Sachs, Lehman Brothers, and the New York Stock Exchange. All around us people were losing their jobs and moving out of the city to save money.

At Little Pim, sales slowed but didn't stop. I felt incredibly lucky. I was grateful I had made the entrepreneurial leap when I did. While leaving the nonprofit world had felt like a very risky decision, I now learned that at my old job they were laying off people in droves, so I actually had more job security, not less. Darren had accepted a position running a community center in downtown New York and, as a huge side benefit, took Emmett to preschool for free where he worked.

While Little Pim was not recession-proof, we knew that one of the last things parents would cut from their budget was their children's education. The recession also made parents suddenly more aware of the importance of a second language in our increasingly global economy. And because our product was reasonably priced, we were not considered a luxury item. We kept selling, and the company's revenues were rising nicely, even if not in a rocket ship kind of way.

Each time I met with John, who was still making introductions to potential funders, he was incredibly encouraging and kept saying, "A recession is a great time to build a business! You can find top talent available for less. And investor expectations are lower."

He was right. We had our pick of many overqualified people to hire. As long as I kept investors informed with my quarterly written updates and phone calls, they seemed not to mind that we hadn't yet hit our initial projections. Some told me that other companies they invested in had actually folded due to the crash. We certainly suffered a decline in sales, but we still kept growing, even if more modestly than we had projected. In addition to the DVDs, we expanded our offerings to include flash cards and music CDs.

It had been a long haul, but there I was, a full-time business owner selling thousands of units of a product that had been just a hunch two years earlier.

I was also exhausted after two years in which I was constantly opening new accounts, creating and executing new marketing campaigns, traveling to trade shows, and finding new investors, all while mothering our two young children. I raised a Series A and a Series B (see glossary) for approximately $1 million each and invested the dollars in marketing, staff, and new products. The business grew, we made over $500,000 in year two, we won over fifteen consumer awards, and we were featured in *BusinessWeek* as one of "America's Most Promising Start Ups." And yet the sales were not generating enough for us to turn profitable or reinvest earned monies in the business. It didn't feel like success. I wanted more. So I looked around for someone who might be able to help me figure out what to do next.

## THE MYTH OF OVERNIGHT SUCCESS

There was only one person in my family who knew about business building: my cousin Justin. He and I both grew up in New York City and both still live here. We are about a year apart in age, were both married with two kids, and were both running businesses in the field of education. Despite our similarities, we weren't in touch very often, except through our mothers' updates.

In the summer of 2011, I was seriously running out of steam. The kind of hockey-stick growth (a slow initial growth followed by a rapid upswing) I had planned for seemed totally out of reach as I sat in my hot office with two full-time staff members, two interns, and a pile of bills that were starting to exceed what we had in the bank account. I still loved creating our products and helping parents give their kids the wonderful gift of a second language, but I was also bone-tired. One morning I woke up with the chilling realization that I was a forty-something mother of two, running a start-up in a six-hundred-square-foot office, facing an uncertain future. I didn't like what I saw in the mirror: a person with big circles under her eyes, increasingly envious of college friends who had chosen more traditional career paths.

To add insult to injury, one of our biggest distributors had just declared bankruptcy, taking $120,000 of our income with them down the drain. It was a crushing loss to a small company like ours. Even worse, I had been the one to negotiate the ill-fated contract. In trying to save on legal fees, I hadn't run it by a lawyer.

That summer I contemplated the benefits of getting out. For the first time, I thought I might have valid reasons to walk away: I wanted to provide for my children, sleep at night, and experience joy at work again. I could sell the company for whatever I could get for it, find a solid job, be able to afford nice vacations again, and escape the mega stress levels that go with being the boss. But in the "You can't quit!" column were all the friends and family from whom I had raised money, not to mention my pride, my love of helping parents be their kids' first language teachers, and my family name. Also, as I had established in middle school, I was not a quitter.

Right around that time, my family grapevine was abuzz with big news: Justin had just sold his company for over $400 million to a media conglomerate. He would have to stay on for a few years to ensure a smooth transition, but his entrepreneurial story seemed to have the happy ending that was eluding me. My mother suggested I call him. At first I put it off, not wanting to seem like I was contacting him only because he had just become the Midas of our family tree. Then again, I reasoned, if I was going to lose face with all my friends and family by selling my business, why not have a huge slice of humble pie first?

I wrote Justin an email congratulating him on the sale of his company and asking if he would consider meeting with me to give me advice about Little Pim. I told him I was considering selling the business. Would he be able to help assess its worth and advise me? To my great relief, he was totally gracious and wrote back right away. Within a few weeks, he was sitting across from me in the middle of our one-room office.

It was a hot August day. Five of us Little Pim-ers—only three of whom were actually on salary—were hunkered down in our cramped quarters. I felt embarrassed that we didn't have a conference room (unless you counted the airless stairwell where I took my private calls) and that the air-conditioning was only half-working. Justin sat across from me in his crisp shirt at our IKEA table with coffee-cup ring marks on it. I asked him to tell me the story of how he had grown and sold his business. The first thing he said was, "You know, it took me ten years to build my business and become an 'overnight success.'"

That was the part of the story my family had left out. Ten years? I had been at Little Pim for six years (two creating the product, four selling), and it was starting to feel like an eternity. But maybe four years of selling wasn't actually that long. In the ten years that Justin had spent building his one business, I had changed careers three times and had two kids. Maybe I wasn't as much of a failure as I'd thought for not having made it yet.

Justin had many questions: about our revenue channels, our margins, and our strategy. Some of his questions I could answer, and some I couldn't. I was working with a part-time accountant who was not in that day, and I didn't know our exact cost of goods for each and every product. Still, Justin got enough out of me to see how it all worked. He was quiet for a few minutes, and then he said in the most matter-of-fact way, "You shouldn't sell this business. You have a great foundation here. You should go raise venture capital and take this company to scale."

Venture capital? I pictured grim-faced men in blue dress shirts and pressed khakis somewhere in Connecticut. Yes, I had raised money, but only from friends and family and various angel investors. It had largely happened over lunch and informal meetings John teed up for me and had required only basic budgets and projections. I had a feeling that pitching to VCs was a totally new, much higher hurdle, and not one I felt prepared to clear.

As Justin started talking about his friends who were VCs or investment bankers and how he knew CEOs who had raised millions of dollars this way, I felt a chill run down my spine. The little I knew about the venture capital world left me thinking these guys were the last people who would understand me or my product, which was created by and for parents and their children. I didn't speak the VC language and feared they would ask me tough financial questions I couldn't answer. Ones like Justin was asking today. No way.

Justin said raising venture capital wasn't that different from raising other kinds of capital. He said investors were interested in businesses that had the potential to go to scale (to make a big return from a relatively small initial investment). He could make introductions and help me through it. I thanked him and said I would think about it.


## DOOR NUMBER THREE

The more Justin's advice ran through my head, the more I knew he was right. I'd thought there were just two doors: run myself into the ground trying to grow my business with only modest resources, or get out. He had shown me door number three: raising venture capital.

In talking to him, I also realized something critical: I wasn't tired of my business; I was just tired of running it like a fledgling start-up. When I imagined having money to hire top-level staff and deploy a sizable marketing budget, suddenly I felt reenergized. I wasn't *done*. I was just done running a small-scale business where I had to wear eight hats each day and also do the dishes in the office sink. What I didn't know yet is that opening door number three was going to force me to face every insecurity I had about myself as a business person.

When I presented the idea of raising venture capital to my board, they were very supportive. By then the board had grown to five people: two angel investors (Marion and Steve), an industry expert in sales and marketing who was a Harvard Business School grad, a partner of John's at his hedge fund, and me. They agreed it was time to get real resources behind the company and offered to help with the documents and budgets we would need to create them.

Around the same time, I learned that a competitor in the kids' space was planning to launch a children's foreign language–teaching product. That sealed the deal. When I imagined another company reaping the spoils of the market we had painstakingly created and where we had been the first movers, I was incensed. The phrase that kept running through my head was *I will not let them eat my lunch!* I realized that one of the only ways to play defense was to raise enough money to play offense.

But I still hated the idea of putting myself into rooms where I had to sell to men whom I doubted would have any real interest in my business. Part of the reason I had become an entrepreneur was to have control over my own work life and choose with whom I worked. To me, VCs were from another planet. I remembered back when I was a nonprofit fundraiser and had to meet with Ed, a top executive in a prestigious growth capital firm. He kept me waiting for over an hour in his glossy reception room in Greenwich, Connecticut. Ed finally ushered me briskly into his office and gestured for me to sit. Then he looked at his watch and said, "You have eleven minutes. Go."

The idea of going back into rooms where I was going to be judged and evaluated by guys like Ed, my business dissected and possibly rejected, conjured up huge fears about failure and embarrassment. I thought, *What if I can't raise the money? What if I fail? I could lose my entire company, let down my employees, and squander the investments family and friends made in my company— investments they made in* me? I realized that to move forward, I needed to find a way to let go of that terror.

Eventually I found a way forward, and I am going to get to just how I did that. But first, I want to pause here and say I get that not everyone has a cousin Justin. In the following chapters I will help you ask yourself some of the same key questions Justin asked me. I'll help you assess *your* business and whether you have considered all the ways you can take it farther faster, with or without raising capital. You can also take my free assessment at juliapimsleur.com. Some of the key questions include:

1.  Are you thinking big enough? Where could your business go if you had twice the resources?
2.  What part of your business might be scalable?
3.  What would more money provide your business? What would running your business "at scale" (at its full potential) look like?

## Chantel Waterbury of Chloe + Isabel

COURTESY OF CHANTEL WATERBURY / PHOTO BY TOMMY NORTHCUT

Chantel Waterbury's company, based in New York City, sells jewelry online across America through hundreds of women micro-entrepreneurs. She created Chloe + Isabel after a carefully plotted fifteen-year career developing jewelry lines for some of the biggest names in the retail world, including Macy's and Target Corporation, and learning the business from all angles. Her interest in direct selling started early: she paid her way through college selling steak knives. She wrote her business plan while on maternity leave. She initially raised $3 million in seed capital and ultimately over $32 million in four different rounds. Her company is valued at over $100 million today.

***How did you prepare for being an entrepreneur—or did you?***

I don't ever like to be comfortable. Starting to feel comfortable means I am not being challenged. You need to understand when you are no longer growing in a role. And take risks. How could I make myself appealing to these companies if I didn't actually know what they wanted? Once, when I was working for a huge retailer I wanted to take a risk on a new product, and when I asked if it was okay, my CEO said, "Chantel, it is better to ask for forgiveness than permission." As women, we want to ask for permission. But from then on I didn't. Multiple times, if I had been wrong, I would probably have been fired. Luckily, the big risks I took always resulted in big rewards. That year I ended up getting Buyer of the Year!

***How did you figure out how much money you would need for your own company?***

I came from an industry where people play in big dollars. It is almost Monopoly money! I managed businesses that ranged from $50 million to $350 million. So when it came time to launch Chloe + Isabel, I initially thought that I was going to need $10 million. I was planning on getting it from CEOs or retail executives, combined with some strategic partnerships with factories. I had always been very careful on how I left each company—I always tried to do it on a high note, leaving the door open. I developed meaningful relationships with CEOs and with executives and that really paid off when it was time to fundraise.

**What made you decide the time was now?**

What made me actually, finally make the leap was getting pregnant, and then my mom dying. It was a combination of those two things, where it was like "What are you waiting for? Just get this done." I wrote a business plan while on maternity leave.

**How did you find your investors?**

My husband was director of national sales for an Internet start-up and happened to mention to his boss, "My wife is working on this business plan." To his surprise she said, "I would love to talk to your wife." Very quickly after we spoke, she offered to introduce me to a friend who was a female VC at a very large firm. And so I went for a meeting. But I was extremely naïve. The venture world was quite foreign to me, so I was quickly given advice to connect with a great lawyer. He ultimately made the introductions where I found the right investment partners. When I was debating between taking venture money versus "strategic" or industry money, he gave me the advice to take "smart money" because it would be able to help in areas—particularly when it came to technology—where the industry money could fall short. And it was the best advice that I ever got.

**How did your pitch meetings go?**

I went in with a PowerPoint presentation. That was it. I had not designed a single piece of product. And I was still working full-time. Everyone thought I was asking for too much money. I remodeled it a million times to see if I could do it with just $1.8 million in initial funding, and it just wouldn't work. I tried to explain, "You are setting me up to fail."

### How did you convince them that it was bigger than that?

The way that I pitched it was never about jewelry. It was always about innovating on direct sales. I showed the size of the industry: $167 billion. I wrote the business plan around the opportunities. I was in my mid-thirties; jewelry just wasn't enough for me anymore. I love jewelry, don't get me wrong, but am I waking up every single day inspired to go and design a new necklace? No. I wanted something bigger that I could be passionate about. These merchandisers, these women, they drive me every single day. I think about Avon. Avon was founded 125 years ago. Imagine, in the late 1800s, a woman getting the opportunity to be a CEO running a business. She couldn't even vote.

### Is it ever hard being the only woman in the room?

The biggest thing that I had to overcome was finding my voice with investors. Women can be so accommodating! When I started, I was avoiding conflict so much that I was allowing myself to get pushed around to a certain extent. It would be like "Okay, I should just do what they say. I don't want to disappoint them. I don't want them to lose their money." Then I realized, "What matters more: that I am pleasing them or that this company succeeds?" It's my job to make sure that we don't run out of money. I need to provide a clear vision and I need to hire the best people and act quickly if it is not working out—and the latter part is easier said than done. Some of my biggest regrets were not letting go of people quickly enough.

### How do you find the support you need?

It is important to remove negative people from your life. What you need is to surround yourself with people who believe. You can't have doubts as a founder. The people who worked really closely with me at my former jobs have told me, "I am so proud of you" and "I knew this was going to happen." All of my bosses were like "Oh, Chantel, we can't wait to see what you do."

# 2

# POWERFUL AND PREPARED, NOT PRETTY AND PERFECT

When it comes to thinking big about our businesses, although we had the drive and will to create a business from nothing (no small feat), we may still be playing small in ways we haven't yet realized. My friend's ten-year-old daughter, Meredith, brought this home to me on a recent weekend getaway when we were playing Boggle.

Boggle is a popular word game in which you and several other players look for hidden words in a jumble of letter cubes and write them down for points, trying to come up with as many words as you can before the three-minute timer is up. Then you compare your list with the other players' and cross off the ones you both have. You only get points for words that are on your list and no one else's.

Meredith learned quickly; she is precocious and very verbal. After just a few rounds, she was coming up with high-scoring words and generally acing it. I pointed out her Boggle prowess to her parents and could tell she was feeling good that an adult was evangelizing about her smarts. We played over and over and had a great time as she found increasingly high-scoring and complex words.

The next day her brother, who was twelve, and my son, who was nine, decided they wanted to play with us too. They had both played Boggle before but weren't particularly strong players. They immediately started playing the game very differently from Meredith. They were guessing wildly at words—writing down words they had completely made up, in the hopes they were right, whereas Meredith wrote down words only when she was completely sure of them. When the boys got a word wrong, they didn't really care; in fact they thought it was funny to push the limits. "Is 'nayvre' a word?" they would ask. "Why not? Let's look it up!" And so on.

On the first round, Meredith held her own. But in the second round, the boys had all the words Meredith did, so she got no points. As she sat next to me on the couch, I saw her little face darken. She pulled her knees up into her chest.

"I am so bad at this!" she said loudly.

"You are not," I countered. "Remember you found the word 'provoke' yesterday for five points and you beat me two times? This was just a tough round."

But she didn't seem able to hear me and continued scowling.

By contrast, when the boys' words were crossed off at the end of a round, they pumped their fists in the air, high-fived each other, and whooped, laughing, "Oh yeah, another zero!"

After one more round in which she got only two points, Meredith took her pen and angrily crossed out every word on her page. Then she declared, "I am never playing this again!" and walked away. I was unable to help her through her frustration, and no amount of reasoning could get her to return to the game.

Meredith's response, in a nutshell, is what happens to many women when we go up against challenge and failure. We would rather not play if we can't get it right. And this creates a situation in which, all too often, women are sitting on the sidelines while men are in the game—not because we are not strong players, but because we find the prospect of failure intolerable.

This attitude is the very antithesis of what makes entrepreneurs able to succeed. My favorite definition of an entrepreneur is this: "Someone who fails and gets up and keeps going." Entrepreneurs are not smarter, more ambitious, or more talented than anyone else. What we have is the ability to take knocks and get back up again quickly—and then find another way forward. We have a kind of Teflon coating that protects us from the sticky gunk that comes flying our way.

One of the reasons women sometimes sit on the sidelines is that, like Meredith, we like to be 99 percent sure we have the right answer before we respond to a question. It is part of what I call our "pretty and perfect" socialization. Despite a very positive shift I have seen toward praising girls for their actions, not their looks, these old stereotypes are still with us. Twenty- and thirty-somethings who are running businesses today were likely still raised at a time when most boys were encouraged to play sports and learned to contend with repeated failure, while most girls were praised for knowing the right answer, pleasing grown-ups and teachers, and being cooperative.

## SELF-LIMITING BELIEFS

When I work with other women entrepreneurs and mention that I struggled with my own self-limiting beliefs before being able to raise money, I always get a lot of "Amen, sister" head nodding. We each have different beliefs to contend with, but we all seem to have stories we tell ourselves about what we can and can't do. This set of beliefs, which sometimes takes the form of paralyzing internal chatter, comes from years of socialization to be pretty and perfect. We were often socialized to please adults instead of being encouraged to be bold and risk-taking. The good news is that these beliefs are not as intractable as they might appear. We can learn to shed behavior and beliefs that no longer serve us and replace them with empowering ones.

**The Five Most Common Self-Limiting Beliefs among Women Entrepreneurs**
1. "If I fail it will be disastrous, so I won't risk too much."
2. "I can't run a multimillion-dollar company because I don't have the business experience."
3. "I won't be able to have a personal life if I am the boss," or "I'll seem too domineering and men won't want to go out with me," or "My husband will resent my spending so much time away from home."
4. "I couldn't do something big like that alone. I would need a cofounder to take the business to scale—ideally a man who's good at the numbers side of things."
5. "Someone else would do a better job than I would."

Do any of these sound familiar? One thing you can do to start whittling away at the power of your own self-limiting beliefs is to say them aloud, write them down, and come up with their positive opposites. There is something about seeing them on paper that helps you realize they are not the truth; they are merely ideas you've held on to and have built a fortress around. Once you see your limiting beliefs in all their absurd and infuriating glory, you can begin to take away their power. You may also realize that these notions you have about yourself were useful in getting you to where you are today, but may be impediments to getting where you want to be tomorrow. See the exercises for this chapter for some help tackling your own limiting beliefs.

I like to imagine that the work I've done to eliminate my own self-limiting beliefs makes me a bona fide "belief buster." Here is what worked for me, and how you can put it to work for you and become a belief-buster for yourself and your friends.

### The Four Essential Steps to Busting Self-Limiting Beliefs
1. Acknowledge the beliefs that are holding you back.
2. Get the self-limiting beliefs out of your head by writing them down.
3. Fill all the newly freed-up space in your brain with new skills and the positive opposite beliefs of the ones you got rid of.
4. Get active in embodying the change (and get ready to go outside your comfort zone).

I'll walk you through each of these steps, but let's start by taking a closer look at our fear of failure. Fear of failure is like fuel on the fire of self-limiting beliefs.

## MY EARLY FAILURE SET ME FREE

In a way, the best thing that can happen to you as an entrepreneur is to fail early on, so it doesn't loom ahead of you as some horrible pitfall to be avoided at all costs. I was fortunate to have failed pretty spectacularly in my twenties in a way that helped me to develop mental toughness and an ability to continue to take risks.

When I was twenty-four and attending graduate school for filmmaking in Paris, I came up with the idea of a guidebook that I thought was sure to be an industry bestseller. The guide would allow Hollywood producers and European screenwriters to find each other, and the producers to option and produce the writers' scripts. There had been a series of Hollywood remakes of European films, like *Cousins* and *Three Men and a Baby*, and I knew from working on international coproductions and my script-reading job at Studio Canal + (a kind of French Universal Studios) that American screenwriters were in demand, but Europeans didn't know how to find them, short of going to Hollywood themselves. This was in the nineties, so international travel wasn't cheap. And there was no Internet to connect the continents easily.

I was so convinced that a guidebook would become a must-have tool on every film executive's desk that I invested hundreds of dollars in a mock-up of the guide, signed up more than fifty writers, and flew to Hollywood for my summer vacation, where I rented a room in an aging burlesque singer's apartment near Sunset Boulevard. I formed a company called Script Source and called all the big talent agencies that represented writers—ICM, William Morris, and CAA—and drove my tin-can rental car to meet with them and pitch the idea.

To my surprise and delight, they took the meetings, were very receptive, and seemed intrigued. I got two or three of them to sign on and promise me a flow of screenwriters. I remember explaining that we would keep the guide up to date by faxing new pages to producers when new scripts were available. Faxes, oy! It's both funny and painful to remember how sure I was this would work.

At the end of that summer, I went back to Paris and kept trying to push my guidebook idea forward while attending classes and working as a script reader, bending the ear of anyone I could get to listen. I continued to pour my hard-earned francs into mock-ups of Script Source, convinced it would pay off in the end. I tried to find a publisher, but I wasn't getting anywhere.

A well-connected professor of mine had a colleague who liked my idea and agreed to pitch Script Source to the European Union Commission for a grant. I was running low on my own funds, and this was my Hail Mary pass, so I spent a few hundred dollars of my dwindling savings on a high-end set of mock-ups, assembled them all by hand, and shipped them overnight at great expense to ten European delegates meeting in Spain. I held out hope for several weeks, but finally got word that no, I had not gotten the grant. The commission didn't see promoting American-European collaborations as a proper use of government funds.

By then I had been working on Script Source for over a year, had spent all of my savings, was the president of the legal entity I had created for the guide that now owed taxes in California, and was pretty darn demoralized. I then made one of the hardest decisions of my life: I decided to fold Script Source and move on. I was about $5,000 in debt, and this project was depleting all my time, energy, and joy. I had a strong feeling that no matter how badly I felt doing a professional face-plant, if I didn't cut my losses it would only get worse. I also thought something better might be around the corner but I wasn't going to find it while staying up until 3 a.m. making mock-ups of a guidebook no one seemed to want. I had not yet heard the famous advice for start-ups that is one of the cornerstones of the Lean Start-Up movement: that it's better to fail faster—meaning, if something isn't going to work, it's better to find out quickly and move on before you spend too much money or human capital. But if I had, it would have been small comfort, because I felt like a total failure. Here I was, this straight-A student who had arguably never screwed up anything big in her life (notwithstanding hosting the first party with booze and no adult supervision in eighth grade), and I was going to tell friends, family, and professors that my idea was going nowhere.

I started by telling my close friends and then eventually informed everyone involved—professors who had encouraged me, the screenwriters who agreed to be part of the first guide, and graphic designers who had done all the design work for free—that Script Source was defunct. People weren't as shocked or disdainful as I had feared. Some even told me they admired the perseverance with which I had gone after my dream. What I learned from their reactions was that my failure did not define me. I got to experience viscerally that my idea was not the sum total of who I was. I cried on my best friend's shoulder, drank too much red wine (thankfully cheap in France), and went back to my studies. I finished graduate school with honors and having produced five short films, including one that won a French human rights award and secured international distribution. I had failed at the company but succeeded in many other areas, and this helped me to put it all in perspective.

I think the most important part of that public failure was realizing that my friends and family still valued and respected me whether my project was a hit or a miss. If they loved me when I was downright *failing*, then perhaps the failure pit wasn't as deep as I thought it was. I could dig myself out and walk again.

Years later I read in *Daring Greatly* what Brené Brown said about the challenge of separating yourself from your work, and it resonated deeply with me: "You want folks to like, respect, and even admire what you've created, but your self worth is not on the table. You know you are far more than a painting, an innovative idea, an effective pitch, a good sermon or a high Amazon.com ranking. . . . This is about what you do, not who you are." She says if you can master this ability to put yourself out there and also remember that your work doesn't *define* you, then you have one of the key ingredients needed to join the "daring greatly" strivers. As she puts it, "Regardless of the outcome, you've already dared greatly, and that's totally aligned with your values; with who you want to be."[1]

When I faced professional risks later in life, I often thought back to Script Source and how it felt to keep going despite that awful feeling of not getting the A (or even a C). This visceral experience of failure is a huge part of what has given me the ability to do my own version of "daring greatly" and take even bigger risks, such as founding my documentary film production company a few years later, called Big Mouth Productions. My best friend from college, Katy Chevigny, and I had only about $3,000 between us when we launched it, but we were passionate about making documentaries that address pressing social issues. "What is the worst thing that can happen?" I remember thinking, as Katy gave notice at her job and I filled out incorporation documents to create our company. I knew from Script Source (1) that if I pursued a big idea with gusto, people would take me seriously (after all, the Hollywood agents took meetings with me); (2) how to push an idea forward (map it out, talk it up to everyone); and, most important, (3) that my people really do have my back.

Thomas Edison captured how essential it is to be able to fail. When asked how he came up with his world-changing inventions, he said, "I failed my way to success." Sara Blakely, founder of the tushy- and tummy-flattening undergarment empire Spanx, grew up with her entrepreneur father asking his kids each night at the dinner table, "What did you fail at today?" He wanted to send the message to his family, and especially his daughter, that failing is just part of life. Failing should be shared and celebrated because it means you are trying new things. Apparently that worked for Blakely, because she failed at not one but two careers before she launched Spanx with a $5,000 investment. Spanx now makes more than $250 million in revenues and sells to more than twelve thousand stores in fifty countries.[2] Blakely was also the first woman to sign the Gates/Buffet "Giving Pledge" and is donating her billion-dollar estate to charity.

## WHAT SELF-LIMITING BELIEFS ARE HOLDING YOU BACK?

Since I had failed early, the challenge for me as a CEO lay mostly in learning to think of myself as a "business person" rather than a "hardworking creative person." Being good at multitasking and having stamina were useful in the early days of my business, when I had to do four different jobs and be ready to fill in whenever I was needed. But raising venture capital required something different: the ability to paint a grand vision for potential investors and project certainty.

Since the early days of founding Little Pim, other business people had often reacted to my idea by saying something like "That could be really big!" I thought so too, but in our first three years of sales we grew only moderately, and I began to wonder why we weren't yet "really big." I also began to seriously question my abilities as a leader. If we hadn't yet become a multimillion-dollar business, was it because I was holding us back?

When I looked inward to try to quiet these anxious thoughts, I saw in myself someone who did well in school, took some early risks, and had big plans and dreams. I also saw someone with persistent insecurities. I kept coming back to the unsettling feeling that I might be standing in my own way. I couldn't point to anything outside of me, like a tyrannical boss, holding me back. It was actually *me* undermining my own ability to lead. I also suspected this might be a very female thing to do. Then I remembered a flagrant example of this that I had stumbled on some twenty years earlier. In my senior year at college, I produced a student documentary called *Boola Boola, Yale Goes Coed*, about the twentieth anniversary of coeducation at Yale. ("Boola Boola" is the Yale football cheering song played after touchdowns.) To make the film, I tracked down and interviewed ten of Yale's first women undergraduates and asked about their experiences at what had been a proudly all-male undergraduate institution for over two centuries.

These Yale women pioneers admitted on camera that once they got over the elation of being selected from among thousands of highly qualified applicants and arrived on campus, they felt variations on "I'm not really supposed to be here." As one alumna put it, "Everyone else was so smart. I was just a regular person."

The Yale Admissions Committee had painstakingly chosen these amazing women to be part of the first coed class, and they were truly *la crème de la crème*. They went on to have brilliant careers in business, journalism, and law. But still, at Yale and maybe beyond, they suffered from what is commonly known as "imposter syndrome," that sense that you're not qualified to be where you are and may get found out at any moment.

During the start-up years at Little Pim, I too suffered from imposter syndrome. Understanding the various finance documents and trying to determine margins on our products put a serious strain on my math abilities. I had never before run a company that had the goal of making money. When I was running my film production company, the goal was ensuring that our films had a wide social impact. Now I had investors who had one goal: a return. Could I really make this company generate millions of dollars per year? Did other CEOs have the secret to turning their ideas into gold?

These internal questions became increasingly loud in my head as the years went by and the company grew but did not become the multimillion-dollar business I had promised. When I first launched Little Pim I was playing to my strengths, drawing on my film and language-teaching background. Once the products were launched, it was time to focus on selling. I was the chief sales person for the first two years, and then brought in a sales director by raising additional monies to pay her. With my sales director, a marketing manager, and a few interns, we had taken the company from $58,000 a year to $500,000 in revenues in three years, but now we needed to double that again and then again.

Negative chatter kept percolating in my brain: *What if I'm not smart enough to pull this off? What if the board asks me to walk them through the profit and loss statement and I don't say the right things?* That kind of anxiety was *not* going to make me enticing to new investors. I had to rewire my brain and create a new, braver soundtrack in my head.

This is a problem that plagues so many women entrepreneurs: How can we tame those voices that say we're not smart enough, forceful enough, or polished enough to go big or attract capital? These limiting beliefs are like huge invisible jugs of water we carry around on our head. We have to concentrate so much on not spilling any water that we wind up taking baby steps. And because we move forward gingerly and cautiously, we keep looking down at our feet instead of up, toward the future.

## THE MINI-STORAGE SELF-IMPROVEMENT PLAN

In my quest to extinguish my own self-limiting beliefs, I found inspiration in an unlikely place: the New York City subway. I kept seeing this ad campaign for a mini-storage facility, encouraging you to pack away items you really didn't need that were cluttering up your probably tiny apartment. I remember musing that it would be so nice if you could pack up your limiting beliefs too and put them into mini-storage along with your old yearbooks. Then I thought, *Well, why not?* Since the thoughts weren't real, why not put them in a virtual locker?

This mini-storage metaphor worked for me because I didn't think I could *actually* throw away a lifetime of stuff that was holding me back, but I liked the idea that I could park the limiting beliefs I had hoarded about my CEO abilities long enough to raise money and take my company to scale. I focused on picturing my storage locker: it was just across the George Washington Bridge; there was a heavy rolling door that locked, and I had the only key. Whenever I felt those limiting thoughts come up, I banished them to mini-storage and felt light again. It was a huge relief, like how you feel when you have just cleaned out your closet and are looking at all that empty shelf space. I ended up not missing those beliefs, and like so many things we put into storage, I never went back to pick them up.

# REPLACING LIMITING BELIEFS WITH EXPANSIVE BELIEFS

Creating space in your brain by parking undermining thoughts elsewhere is just the first step. The next step is to replace your limiting beliefs with their positive opposites. For example, you may need to replace a limiting belief like "I shouldn't be too outspoken or people will think I'm too aggressive" with a positive version like "I am bold and confident."

Replacing limiting beliefs can be done with a coach, peer group, therapist, or mentor. It is intimate, soul-searching work, so we need to choose our guides carefully. I was able to work with my business coach and advisors on my initial set of self-limiting beliefs that might have prevented me from raising capital. But it's not a "once-and-done" process; I have continued to seek out people to help me get to new levels of confidence and self-awareness so I can be a better leader, mother, and friend.

I found one of my best belief-busting coaches, Gina Mollicone-Long, when she came to speak at EO (Entrepreneurs' Organization), of which I was a member. I was part of a small group that had lunch with her and was immediately drawn to her high energy, successful track record, and confident manner.

Gina travels all over the world helping men and women to break through issues holding them back in their personal and professional lives. She had me hooked when she said, "I can help you get out of your own way." I had been wondering how to do that for years. It felt very much like one of those "when the student is ready, the teacher appears" moments.

One of the things Gina does in her workshops is help people literally and metaphorically break through. She sets up a solid wooden board on two concrete blocks spaced a few inches apart and teaches you how to chop the board in two. *Yeah, right*, we thought when we saw that board. But she quelled our grumbling by showing us that breaking boards is really just a matter of learning to focus all your attention on achieving your goal—in this case, getting your hand to the other side of the board and touching the floor. You focus on the end result, not the obstacle in between. This leads to a great lesson, which is that you can literally break through anything if you have enough desire and let go of your limiting beliefs. I saw men and women go from obsessing over their fear of physical pain to total elation from having broken the board, all in the space of about ten minutes. Gina has helped even very petite women break right through that board, after which they throw their arms up with a "Yeah, I did it!" victory shout. It's exhilarating to watch.

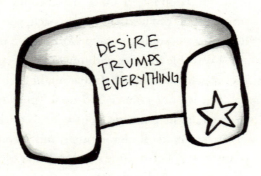

Gina took on only a few private clients a year, and I contemplated being one of them. I spent weeks deliberating about whether I could afford to spend over $10,000 on a private coaching session and learned that many CEOs—men and women—had paid this much for private coaching, and even much more. Gina's references checked out better than well, as people shared the incredible things that had happened in their businesses and personal lives since they had worked with her. I decided I would go for it. The board I believed I needed to break through was whatever was keeping Little Pim from being more successful, something within me. If Gina could help me get closer to spearheading our company's fast-track growth, the money would be well spent.

I flew to Canada in June 2013 to do an intensive one-on-one workshop with Gina at her office in Toronto. She worked with me for two days, using a combination of neurolinguistic programming, Time Line Therapy®, and some Gina-special breakthrough processes. Then she sent me back to New York with several weeks of follow-up exercises to make it stick. The exercises included twenty-one days of daily affirmations—reinforcing statements about myself that I needed to say out loud as part of a morning ritual, such as "I will create my own destiny," and "I am resilient." The point of this exercise was to bring to the fore the internal resources I already had, but had pushed way, way down. We did follow-up phone calls, and she helped me put the change into action. Gina uses the metaphor of a garden to describe her work. First you have a vision for the garden you want (without the weeds of limiting beliefs mucking it up). Then she helps you identify the weeds, remove them, and plant new seeds. After that you still have to water, fertilize, and cultivate the garden until the plants and flowers show up the way you want them to. These daily affirmations and exercises may sound like hooey, and if Gina had told me in advance what I would be doing, I might have said no. But I trusted her, and this mix of interventions and tactics had a profound effect on me.

I had done years of personal therapy, retreats, and leadership workshops that no doubt factored into my being ready. But working with Gina was totally different from any traditional therapy or retreat. Once I started jettisoning those limiting beliefs and living according to new ones, I felt new levels of energy and a real shift occurred. I returned to Little Pim with markedly greater confidence, and we entered into a new line of business that would position us for greater success in the evolving children's language learning and entertainment landscape. I also founded Double Digit Academy, my workshop to help women raise angel and venture capital. I pitched the book idea for *Million Dollar Women* and found a literary agent and publisher in the space of four months. Darren too saw changes in my energy and mood. I was happier and more relaxed, and I had more patience with our boys. For the first time in my life I could see an unobstructed path stretched out before me. Pretty powerful stuff.

But paying a coach to help you break through is not the only way to get rid of your limiting beliefs and start acting like the bolder, more confident version of yourself. Your teacher might be an advisor, a therapist, or a great book. If you can't afford seminars, coaches, and the like or want to start by reading more about it, check out the books in the bibliography and the online resources at juliapimsleur.com.

As part of replacing my limiting beliefs with positive ones, I started adding "yet" to the end of every thought I had about what I could not do, as in "I do not know how to explain our financial projections with authority . . . yet" or "I don't feel confident about getting up and pitching in front of a room full of VCs . . . yet." The "not yet" trick is my favorite way to keep from getting stuck. As an entrepreneur I have signed up for a lifetime of "not yet" because my industry is always changing, along with the means of distribution, marketing tactics, and how our customers find us. Embracing "not yet" just means accepting that you are a lifelong learner.

Once I recalibrated my thinking and carted my limiting beliefs off to mini-storage, I had to make sure my new, better self-conception took root. Gina told me I had to reinforce my new belief that I am good at public speaking by getting out there and doing as much of it as possible. Following her advice, I took every opportunity, from toasts at dinner parties to guest lecturing for college classes to taking the stage at a nonprofit benefit, and it started becoming easier. Soon public speaking became something I actually enjoyed.

## PREPARED, NOT PERFECT

Thanks to Gina, I learned to focus on what I wanted. Thanks to another coach, I learned that I didn't have to be perfect to get it. I met Bill Smartt at a workshop he was leading about improving public speaking skills and liked him so much that I signed up for a set of five private coaching sessions. One day, while he was training me for an upcoming investor pitch, I was getting annoyed with myself for not being able to remember the exact wording of my opening. The third time I said, "Let's start over," he reminded me, "Julia, you want to be prepared, not perfect." Bill explained that your body language and tone of voice actually matter more than what you say. When you are so focused on repeating lines *exactly*, you run the risk of making the talk feel canned and thereby appearing less confident. "It should feel like a conversation you are having with the audience," he said.

Bill also introduced me to research on how people judge the effectiveness of a speaker. According to Albert Mehrabian,[3] a famous researcher on communication, what people remember is the "7-38-55 rule":

- 7 percent content
- 38 percent tone of voice
- 55 percent body language

What you say is less than 10 percent of what people remember! Mehrabian has been quoted as saying the 7-38-55 rule was taken out of context from his research, and it may be exaggerated, but the importance of body language and tone is undisputed. I decided to start focusing more on my tone and how I moved and used my hands when presenting, rather than getting every word just right. Bill's "prepared, not perfect" advice has stayed with me and helped me to curb my perfectionist tendencies, not just in public speaking but also in presenting to my board, negotiating deals, and other high-pressure situations.

One of the best antidotes I've found to this wanting-to-be-perfect paralysis is to channel my anxiety into intensive preparation. When pitching, for example, I do in-depth research on the firm and people I am pitching to and find out information that is not available on the Internet, like who an investor *almost* funded and why it didn't work out. I ask my board members and advisors to run me through practice pitches. I also work with Bill for ninety minutes before every important pitch. He always helps me tighten up my story, improve my delivery, and come up with more inspiring endings. When I focus on how prepared I am—instead of fearing they will call me out on what I don't know—I always feel much calmer and more confident.

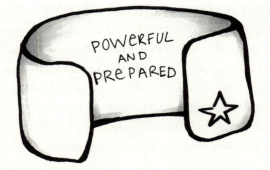

I began noticing that fantastic orators I've had the privilege of hearing, such as the leadership guru Simon Sinek and the author and Barnard College president Debora Spar, often have a moment when they are less than perfect. They fumble a line or go off on a tangent or make a bad joke—and it simply doesn't matter, so long as they keep going and don't let it break their stride.

I took inspiration in shedding perfectionism from my son Emmett too. He was learning to play piano at the same time I was learning to "play" venture capital. He was just eight years old when he decided he wanted to perform a musical piece we both like from the film *Amélie* at my birthday party. It was a high-pressure performance for him, playing in front of twenty adults! The piece started off beautifully, and I was beaming. But I think the part I liked best was when he stumbled and played an audibly wrong note and just kept playing—no apology, no freezing, no starting over. He just kept going and giving it his all. He was grinning with shy pride at the end, when the grown-ups were clapping heartily. I thought, *If he can hold on to that ability to keep going, he can accomplish anything he wants in the world*.

So how do we get to that place of confidence, and silence the voices that tell us we aren't ready for primetime? In her book *Think or Sink*, Gina says that we can force our way out of what she calls "the backward paradigm" by switching some words around. She explains that many people have cause and effect backward. They live in a system of Have-Do-Be that goes something like this: "If I only Had money (or whatever you want) then I could Do what I wanted, and then I could Be happy (or whatever you want)."

The essence of Gina's solution is this: "The cause [of getting stuck] is always internal and the effect is always external. If you practice Be-Do-Have you have a greater chance of getting 'unstuck' and achieving your goals faster. Think about what it would take to 'be' the person you want to be, and start 'do'-ing things that kind of person would do right away. Don't wait, just start, and the changes will come in the doing."[4]

Her theory reminds me of one of the cuffs I slide on when it's time to get out there and do things I am petrified of trying: "Have the fear. Do it anyway."

One way I was able to start practicing Be-Do-Have was to spend more time with business people who were ahead of where I was, through joining Entrepreneurs' Organization (EO) and other networking.

How can you too practice Be-Do-Have? Start by acting like the person you are trying to become (a successful CEO) and watch the changes happen.

- Join a professional organization of entrepreneurs like EO or Vistage.
- Look into the Small Business Office or Women's Business Council in your city or town to find other entrepreneurs and attend free or low-cost workshops.
- Start blogging on issues related to your business. Become a thought leader.
- Do more public speaking. Put yourself in situations where you build those skills.
- Attend workshops, seminars, and talks on business leadership generally and on specific skills you may want to improve, like sales, marketing, and strategy.
- Ask someone you respect to work with you as a mentor or advisor.
- Read books about people who overcame obstacles and what they went through. I loved reading *Daring Greatly* by Brené Brown, who explores how to overcome the fear of going public with your work, and Amanda Palmer's *The Art of Asking*, a

colossal kick in the Spanx when you're hesitating about asking for what you need. You can find more books in the bibliography and at juliapimsleur.com.

## REVIEWING THAT MINI-STORAGE CONTRACT

Before going farther, I want to reiterate the steps I've just described. First of all, realize that failure is inevitable at various points in your entrepreneurial career. That's what being an entrepreneur is: taking chances, falling down, and getting back up again. Keep doing it enough, and eventually you'll get a win that makes it all worthwhile. Second, acknowledge that it's okay to have negative chatter and fears that reinforce your limiting beliefs. But to make space for success, you need to box up those beliefs and cart them off to mini-storage. That leaves room you can fill up with new skills. Coaches, therapists, and peers can help you do this. Third, to make sure it all sticks, practice Gina's Be-Do-Have and get active in moving toward you bigger, bolder self. Once you've done all this, you're primed to lead.

Next you need to make sure the people around you at work and at home will back you up and that you know where to get the skills on your "not yet" list. In the next chapter, I'll talk about identifying your allies and enemies. There's plenty of room in that mini-storage facility to store a few naysayers while you are packing stuff away!

### Brittany Hodak and Kim Kaupe of ZinePak

COURTESY OF ZINEPAK/ PHOTO BY SHERVIN LAINEZ

ZinePak makes custom interactive products for fans of popular music that are sold at retail throughout the United States. When they launched in 2011 with just $60,000, Brittany and Kim often used multiple credit cards to charge orders. Once they were in a financial position where they could start project 4 without waiting to be paid by project 3, the company's growth increased exponentially.

They now have deals with retail giants like Walmart. At that store alone, ZinePak sales have surpassed $30 million. Some of the artists they have featured in their fan products include Katy Perry, Brad Paisley, and Taylor Swift.

### What was it like to start your own company?

**BH:** I think my first Google search was "how to start a company." But I was twenty-six, and I thought, "If there's a time to try and fail, that time is now."

**KK:** We talked a lot about "What if it fails?" I don't think we ever had a conversation in the first year about "What if it's successful?" It wasn't until we hit the first million-dollar-revenue month that we sat back and thought, "This is working."

### Did you encounter any particular issues as young women?

**BH:** Something that I don't think either one of us was prepared for was we would go into a meeting and be speaking with senior people, and they would say, "Oh, this is a great idea. Whose company is it?" And we would say, "It's our company." And they would say, "Right, but who *owns* the company?" And we would say, "We do." This happened everywhere, from major record labels to advertising agencies. It happened every day in the first year—and, as a matter of fact, yesterday. Sometimes we laugh it off and sometimes it's really offensive.

### What's an example of one of those times?

**BH:** I remember the second or third project we did was with a Fortune 500 company. We were in the home office, meeting the people in shopper marketing. They said, "This is so impressive. I want to take you to the home marketing division so you can meet the entire office and we can work together." We were all dressed up in our suits, and we were sitting at the table giving the introduction to the company. A senior vice president in the company raised his hand when we were about five minutes in and said, "Hold on, I'm gonna stop you right there. I need to know which one of your fathers works at Walmart." We were just silent, stunned silent. We had been so nervous about this meeting and we had all this stuff prepared. We just sat there, and you could see the looks on other people's faces of sheer horror. He just couldn't imagine that we had actually gotten this deal on our own.

*How do you stay thinking big?*

**BH:** I think it's a mindset. I remember the day we incorporated our company, the CPA who filed the paperwork for us said, "Are you guys thinking about selling the company soon? Is this short term, long term?" And I said, "We're gonna sell the company for one hundred million dollars." He laughed, and he was like "Honey, your company's not worth anything." I was like "Right, which is why we're not selling it today. But it's worth one hundred million dollars, and that's what we're gonna sell it for." That's been my mentality from before I started the business: I'm not selling this company for less than one hundred million dollars. We meet so many people who give up so much equity so early on. We have been grounded in the big picture since day one. That's why we treat our equity as so precious, because every percentage of equity in our company is worth one million dollars.

*Do you think that being an entrepreneur is harmonious with having a family life, or does that give you pause?*

**KK:** I think it absolutely can be harmonious. But entrepreneurship is super lonely, because your friends lose patience with you when you cancel dinner for the fifth time in a row and miss the third birthday party. There's a lack of understanding about why what you're doing is so important and such a priority all the time. So to surround yourself with other people who are doing the same things that you're doing and have the same passion as you is really great.

**BH:** When I was twenty-seven, I was like "There's no way I will ever be able to have a kid. My business is my baby." My grandparents would be like "When are you gonna have a baby?" I would say, "Well, I do. His name is ZinePak. He's eleven months old." And now that I'm a little bit older and more of my entrepreneurial peers are having babies, I'm like "Oh yeah, I can do that too." It's easier to wrap my head around.

# 3

# IDENTIFY YOUR ALLIES, YOUR FOES, AND YOUR FRENEMIES

When I go to parties and meet new people, there is one conversation I have over and over again. It's my own personal Groundhog Day, and it goes like this:

*Jill or Jim:* So, what do you do?

*Me:* I run a company that introduces young children to a second language via a multimedia series.

*Jill or Jim:* How interesting! I was so bad at Spanish! So, do you run the business out of your home?

*Me (forced smile, internal wincing):* Actually, we're a staff of eight with distribution in twenty-two countries. Our offices are in Union Square.

I guarantee I would not be getting that question over and over if I were a man. But because I'm a woman and a mother, people assume that my business is something cute and little that I squeeze in while my kids are at school.

So many female entrepreneurs I've met and coached have stories like this. We have to fight to keep all these well-meaning but ultimately undermining people out of our heads—and, in extreme cases, our lives. We also need to find people who know that what we are trying to do does not warrant "Oh, how sweet!" but "Wow, that sounds promising! How big are you planning to go with it?"

Especially in the vulnerable early stages of a business, and again as you are trying to hit ambitious new milestones, you need smart, supportive people around you. Have you ever heard the saying "You are the average of the five people you spend the most time with?" The first time I heard that it really made me stop and think. I had already hired highly competent people at work, but what was the state of my entourage outside of work?

When I got serious about building my business, I decided I needed to put myself into situations—work, social, and a bit of both—that would help me find people who would both cheer me on and challenge my thinking in new ways. I needed to find peers and business people who were a few steps ahead of me and would help me grow in the areas where I needed help, such as staff management, long-term company planning, and fundraising.

So many women entrepreneurs credit their success and the rapid growth of their companies to having the right people in their corner. Take Chantel Waterbury, the CEO of Chloe + Isabel, the direct-to-consumer jewelry sales company whose story I shared earlier in the book. She has raised $32 million and created a twenty-first-century version of the Avon model of selling, helping women become micro-entrepreneurs selling jewelry online. Chantel knew in her early twenties that she wanted to eventually launch her own business. She carefully and intentionally cultivated mentors, friends who believed in her, and field experts throughout the fifteen years she spent at retail giants like Macy's, J.Crew, and GAP, Inc. By the time she launched Chloe + Isabel she had people cheering her on, saying, "I know you can do this!" and offering connections and strategy advice.

As a CEO, you need to be a fountain of optimism and inspiration for your team. One of your most important roles is to do what I call "holding the vision" for where your company is headed, no matter how many twists and turns it takes to get there, so it's critical to surround yourself with positive people who will help you stay in that "do see" mindset. I still spend time with friends who like to point out all the things that could go wrong, but we're on more of a twice-a-year-for-coffee schedule, and with them I steer away from talking about my business. Some of the people in my life were either too risk-averse themselves to cheer me on, or they just emphasized the risks in an unhelpful way.

"Surrounding yourself with people—especially entrepreneurs—who are more successful than you and who have also had their ass kicked a few times and are still more successful than you, that really helps you when you are going through the lulls," says my friend Christel Caputo, the founder and CEO of Couch Busters International (CBI), a successful job-placement agency. "You know, when you are thinking, 'I don't think I can do this. Maybe I'm not the entrepreneur I thought I was. Maybe this was all

luck'? At those times it's especially good to tap into those who have come before you or who are in the fight." Brené Brown calls those of us who are engaged in doing something big, bold, and sweaty-making "people in the arena" (from a famous speech by Theodore Roosevelt) and she reminds us that we have more in common with one another than the folks who are "in the bleachers" and are often the biggest critics from their safe seats.[1]

We all have cheerleaders and naysayers in our lives—and we usually don't get to choose which ones are in our family. I was talking with a fellow entrepreneur, Stacey Brook, about naysayers and what to do when they are in your close circle, like your family. She runs a company called College Essay Advisors that helps high school kids ace their college essays. Stacey says her entire family, and her parents in particular, have been hugely supportive of her company, but for some reason her mother has never liked the colors of her company logo. Stacey recently designed an infographic that she was super excited to start using. "I didn't show it to my mother in advance," she said, "because I knew that no matter what good things she might have to say about it, she would also tell me, as she always does, that she hates my brand colors, something I do not want to do anything about." Sure enough, when Stacey's mom saw the new image, she said, "It's great. Can I just say one thing, though?"

We can't always choose who is around us; however, we can choose not to take in what they say. My dear friend Tanya came up with a saying that is now one of my favorite mantras and has been a huge help to me in staying positive during the past twenty years. Here it is:

Next time you catch yourself getting pulled down by naysayers, grab this cuff and create your own Wonder Woman defense field. I am not suggesting you should act without integrity or provoke others intentionally, but as women we often get caught up in what other people think of us in a way that is unhelpful and even paralyzing at times.

## FRIENDS WHO INSPIRE

The important thing is that *you* know why you are building your business and can find others who are also on big, bold journeys that require similar tenacity and temerity. An extremely small percentage of the world's population ever try to be entrepreneurs, so some people might think you are weird, based on that alone. And you *are* different, based on that alone. Just own it and move on. Cultivating a circle of people who help shore you up is just as important as picking the right images for your products or the right programmers for your website.

Recently I ran into my friend Melanie, whom I hadn't seen in a few months. For the five years I have known her, Melanie always had beautiful, straight brown hair that fell below her shoulders. This time her hair, though still long, was super curly. I complimented her on the new look.

"You know," she said brightly, "a few months ago I decided to launch a business. I really want to combine philanthropy with online gifting. But we need the dual income, and I am not going to be able to give up my job anytime soon. I looked at everything I do, between the kids, work, and training for marathons, and realized if I stopped blow-drying my hair I could find an extra thirty minutes a day to work on my business!"

I just love how positive and resourceful women can be when they want to make something happen. I think of Melanie often when I want to get something done and think I just don't have time—or when I choose to write a blog or set up a playdate for my kids in the window of time usually allotted for grooming!

The people you have in your corner don't have to be entrepreneurs like you. They just have to be "in the arena." They can be undertaking a big career change or trying to up their game professionally. They can be people you spend time with in person or via videoconferencing.

Stacey of College Essay Advisors says that in the early days of her business, she brainstormed with her personal trainer, who became a good friend (all while helping her have great abs). Christel of CBI says that in the early days of her business, she had weekly check-ins with a friend who was a lawyer: "He is very sure of himself, and I like seeing the way he thinks in the guys' work world, his enthusiasm and his passion for his own craft."

Research has shown that people who work with others to reach their goals have a higher chance of success, as we have seen in companies that harness the power of collective pursuits, like Fitbit and Weight Watchers.[2] All around you are amazing women and men with their own dreams and plans. If you can gather one or two of them, you can help keep each other on track and reach your goals faster. Some people meet informally; others choose to form mastermind or accountability groups, where two to five people meet regularly, setting thirty-, sixty-, and ninety-day goals for which they hold one another accountable. When I was in an accountability group with my friend Mark, we would each email up a storm the night before a meeting so we could say we'd done the things on our lists. He was my support system for over a year, and we both deepened our friendship and made important life decisions during the year we met monthly and kept each other on track.

I also want to touch on frenemies—people you thought were friends but who actually behave more like the opposite when it comes to helping you achieve your dreams. Christel described a friend she had to distance herself from because the friend was constantly implying that Christel hadn't yet paid her dues: "I didn't go to the same amount of school or take the classes that she did, and I didn't take the same licensing exam. I went down a path that was different than hers. I think she feels that because of all the time and energy she's put into her education to get this one particular degree, it's like I'm completely swiping it away and it's all illegitimate if I'm walking into her industry." Not surprisingly, the relationship cooled.

Heather Willems, CEO of ImageThink, a design company that creates graphic recordings of events and meetings, says she is super choosy about friends she spends time with outside of work, in part because she feels she can't really let her hair down at work: "When I came into the role of boss and a business owner, I felt like I had to be on guard and tough and have all the answers. Especially in this world, where so many business owners are men, I feel like I have to be on my game all the time!" When she's off the clock, she needs to recharge with friends who believe in her and the business.

## Denise Wilson of Desert Jet

Denise Wilson is the founder, president, and CEO of Desert Jet, which provides private jet charters and jet aircraft maintenance. Desert Jet has been on the Inc. 500|5000 list of the nation's fastest-growing privately owned companies four years in a row and is one of the few women-owned private jet companies in the United States. Denise founded the company as a pilot; running a company that earns multimillion-dollar revenues gives her the freedom to travel, give back to the community, and mentor women in the aviation industry.

### How did you find your way into the jet industry?

My first career was as a professional oboist and music teacher. Looking for a hobby outside of music, I learned to fly and fell in love with aviation. I left music and became a professional pilot. I progressed into a position as an airline captain; then September 11 wreaked havoc on the airline industry and I lost my job. With the airlines furloughing at the time, I was lucky to find work in business aviation, flying a private jet for a high-net-worth individual. Once the airlines started hiring again I was hired by Aloha Airlines to fly the Boeing 737 on interisland routes. But after sixty-two years of being in business, Aloha folded almost overnight. I soon learned that the aviation industry was not going to provide me with stability and that if I wanted to remain a pilot, I was going to have to get resourceful. That's when I decided to start my own aviation company and take control of my destiny.

### When you started the company in 2007, what capital did you have?

I had no capital to begin with. I bartered with aircraft owners to let me use their planes, and then I paid them after I got paid. When I started, I was working with one jet plane owner. Now there are nine. In our first year we made $787,000. Last year we made $11 million, and we are still growing.

**How did you learn the business?**

The operational side was easy as I had significant experience as a pilot. As far as running a business, it was all new to me, and I had to just learn it on my own. I researched a lot on the Internet and read books about marketing. I learned how to do accounting and the myriad other tasks that were required. Later, as I hired employees, I was able to pass along what I had learned.

**How did you get your confidence?**

Building this business has made me stronger and more optimistic overall. When things get tough, which they do when starting a business, you almost have to feign optimism just to keep yourself going after each knockdown. I think being persistent and always knowing that things will get better is an absolute must. And success begets more confidence, that you're doing it right and that you're on the right track with your plan and vision. You can't have true confidence, though, without being the expert in your field, and I think the operational knowledge I have been able to develop over the years has really helped me believe I can accomplish anything in aviation that I can dream.

## FIND YOUR PEEPS

As you build your business and go outside of your comfort zone to learn new skills, you will need your "peeps" to have your back. With every new year, new product, new iteration of your company come steeper slopes to climb. As I was writing this book about über-successful women, ironically my own company started taking a turn for the worse. We hit a bad quarter, revenues declined radically, and we suddenly realized we needed to change the way we were distributing our product. Though we have always sold DVDs to mass retailers like Toys 'R' Us and Barnes & Noble, the box sets were no longer selling well there, following a drop in DVD sales nationwide, and that was leading to inventory and cash-flow problems. We decided we needed to get out of mass retail, which would mean downsizing staff, changing our projections, and retooling the business. This came at a time when my VP of finance had suddenly left our company for a much better-paying job. I couldn't find a replacement, and I had to get by with a part-time consultant. He was only in a few days a week and was rarely available to answer the many financial questions that the board was lobbing at me.

It all came to a head on yet another fateful hot summer day, this time in August 2014. I got on a conference call with my board. By the time we ended the call, we had all agreed the business needed to be restructured. We were changing sales strategies and focusing on a new line of business in the day care market. It was all happening so fast, and the financial consultant was not in, and my senior VP of sales and marketing was on vacation. The rest of our tight-knit staff had gone home, so I was all alone in my conference room (by then we had a real one!).

I could hardly wait to hang up the phone, as I knew the tears were just seconds from streaming down my face. I lay down on the office couch and cried, because I didn't know the way forward, and I felt I had failed to deliver on the promise of the company. Yes, we had exciting plans in a new sales channel and were developing a cutting-edge day care curriculum that could lead to millions more in revenues. But in that moment I felt I had let everyone down because our sales were down.

Then, mid-snivel, I remembered that I was supposed to show up in twenty minutes at the annual EO summer party, where I had asked to speak publicly. I had recently taken over as the volunteer chair of EO Accelerator and had to pull favors to be able to speak in front of our 220 members at the party. I thought, how am I going to do that?

I placed a call to the one person on the planet I thought could—maybe—get me off that couch. Carrie and I had met only seven months earlier, when she joined EO, but right away we bonded as fellow mom-CEOs who worked hard, loved to laugh even harder, and could own up to our less than perfect selves. Carrie is like a huge heart walking around, holding up an amazing brain, topped with equally amazing hair. She always leads with love but is also smart as a whip, and, as a former chief finance officer, she really knows her numbers.

Carrie answered my emergency text right away and within minutes was on the phone with me. With her irresistible verve, she reminded me that every CEO has faced this kind of pivotal moment at one time or another, that I am not a failure, that I will find a way through this, and by the way, to please send her my financials so she can help me figure out what to do next. "But how can I put on a dress and go to this party and speak in front of everyone?" I sniffed.

"You are going to come to this party," she said in her bubbly but do-not-mess-with-me tone, "and we are going to have a drink, and it's all going to be fine."

Coming from her, it sounded believable, though I really wanted to crawl under the couch. I ventured out of the conference room and put on my bought-for-the-occasion leopard-print dress, squeezed a few drops of Extra-Care Visine into my eyes, doubled up on eye shadow, and got on the subway.

When I got to the party, which was a sun-kissed gathering with amazing views at the tip of Manhattan, I felt a million times better. I was met with warm greetings and handed white wine. I felt a wave of relief wash over me—especially when I spotted not only Carrie but also Victor, an entrepreneur who lost his restaurant two years earlier, when Hurricane Sandy flooded it to bits. He has since rebuilt it with help from all of us in EO, plus is opening a new location. And there was Gary, who had to drop out of EO for a time to retool his business and find a way to increase revenues—and so many others who had risen and fallen so many times. I was deliriously happy they were all there. I knew I belonged among them. I got up and made my speech about the Accelerator program and got several new mentors to sign up. Carrie and I had that drink, and we laughed long and loud.

Everyone needs a Carrie to get through the low lows that are an inevitable part of running a business. In the next chapter I will describe how you can assemble your own professional and emotional infrastructure so that you too can get off the couch—and get to the party.

## 4

# BE LIKE NOTRE DAME,
# NOT THE EIFFEL TOWER

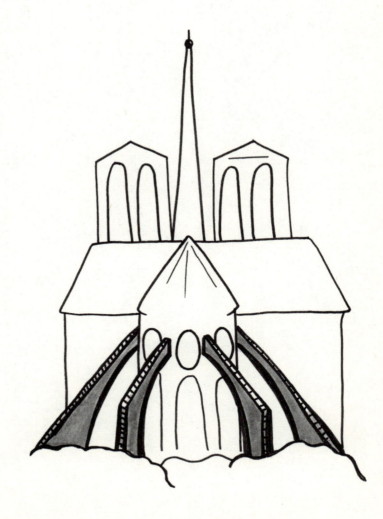

Thinking we need to do it all, know it all, and ace it all is one of the biggest misunderstandings we need to move past in order to take our companies to the $1 million mark and beyond. In fact research has shown that the surest indicator of success in business is not the leader's business track record, the product, the cash on hand, or the industry; it is the leader's ability to set a goal and drive her team toward that goal.[1] That's it. Of course, to make that work, you also need a great team.

Leadership coach Verne Harnish says it best: "Your job as the CEO is not to have all the answers. It's to ask the right questions."[2] We need to assemble the best team to help us answer those questions, and we need to create a structure in which they can thrive.

When I discovered this way of framing leadership, it came as a huge relief and helped me to be a better leader at work, with my board, and in coaching women in my Double Digit Academy. Once I accepted the idea that I was supposed to be more of a conductor than a lead singer, I could relax into feeling proud of what I *was* good at. Then I was able to find the people who had other areas of expertise that would help Little Pim scale up more quickly.

The first few years I was running my business, I had a chip on my shoulder about not having gone to business school. I wasn't good at reading financial spreadsheets, and I often felt ill-equipped to answer finance questions at board meetings. I had run a nonprofit and managed departments of five to ten people, but I had never run a business where the main purpose was generating revenues. Ultimately I had to stop expecting that I would one day wake up and be like the CEOs I read about in *Forbes*. I needed to get comfortable with what I brought to the table that was unique—the positive work culture I had created at Little Pim that attracted top talent and the proprietary and scalable method of language teaching I'd invented—and simply figure out how to get help with the rest. It's like what I taught my son Adrian when he was five years old and learning to tie his shoes: "Focus, and ask for help."

## OUR LADY, NOTRE DAME

One thing that helped me to shift my self-image as a leader was one of the most famous monuments in France: the Cathedral of Notre Dame (which actually means "Our Lady" in French!). I had the good fortune to live in Paris for several years after college. During that time I often rode my bicycle past this world-renowned monument. Considered one of the most beautiful cathedrals in the world, Notre Dame is a classic example of Gothic architecture, with intricately detailed façades and iconic gargoyles. Notre Dame also has something else: twenty-eight visible exterior supporting arches, called "flying buttresses."

Those visible supports do not detract from Notre Dame's beauty. No one ever says, "Nice cathedral. Too bad it needs all those flying buttresses to stay up." In fact the supporting arches not only give the cathedral strength but enhance its beauty.

I decided to take inspiration from Notre Dame for one of my mantras as a business person. I would have as many helpers—my own "flying buttresses"—as I needed to succeed. Like the famous cathedral, these supports would make me and my company stronger and more attractive.

Asking for help sounds like a simple thing to do, but many business owners are more like the Eiffel Tower in this regard. Where Notre Dame is an ode to teamwork, the Eiffel Tower is the ultimate steely solo flyer.

Because men are often still socialized to be Eiffel Tower types, they frequently don't ask for help even when they most need it. You know that won't-ask-for-directions gene that seems to travel on the Y chromosome? It comes up in business too. The ability to ask for help is an area where we women may have a huge advantage over men.

Part of being able to ask for help is having confidence in the unique skill set you bring to the table—and then filling in around it. As entrepreneurs we are often good at putting our staff to their best and highest use and promoting and moving people to jobs that draw on their strengths. But when it comes to our own best and highest use, many of us try to be a Jill of All Trades, and this can hold us back. It may seem like a paradox, but the more you value yourself, the easier it is to ask for help. In my case, I am very clear that I am the creator, the visionary, the champion of our core values, and the language expert in my company. I also know I need to hire people in key roles who are smarter than I am and can teach me—and that I need to draw on advisors and coaches in areas like sales, finance, and strategy.

## PAID COACHES FOR SPOT TRAINING

In addition to working with mentors, advisors, and sponsors as "flying buttresses," I am a big believer in paid coaches who can provide "spot training" in specific areas. When you consider how much is at stake in your business and how much you spend on technology, staff, and production, why wouldn't you invest at least a few thousand dollars a year in coaches for your company's most valuable asset: you?

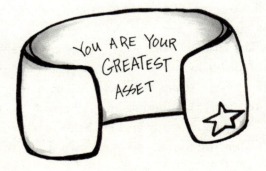

I found my coaches through fellow CEOs, by attending workshops, and by contacting speakers I heard at conferences. Even though some coaches charge hundreds of dollars an hour, most of them have a sliding scale and will often accept a lower hourly rate if you can commit to a block of sessions. I have never regretted the money I spent on a business coach, public speaking coach, or efficiency coach, each of whom can cost between $100 and $300 an hour. I can point to dozens of situations where they helped me achieve a big win, like a new investor, a successful social media strategy, or a better way of structuring my business.

After I raised venture capital, for example, my business coach Steve Nakisher helped me rethink the way I managed my sales team. He flew to New York from Chicago to lead our company's annual day-long strategic retreat and helped me come up with a revised organization chart and new systems for running a multimillion-dollar business. The structures he provided worked. I stopped going to our weekly marketing meetings (which lasted over three hours) and instead met with my senior team once a week for ninety minutes. They sent me written updates to review in advance. Thanks to the new system I could hold us all accountable but not be involved in the minutiae of every marketing campaign. This freed up more time to work with my investors, attend industry conferences, and find new partners.

Entrepreneurs sometimes think "I'll hire a coach when we are making more money," but it's something you need to build into your annual budget from the day you decide to go big. Your ongoing professional development will also have a concrete impact on the company's development. When we went through cash crunches, I would sometimes cut back on coaches or find less expensive alternatives. But I always viewed coaches as an investment in my leadership, and therefore a way of increasing the value of the company even if I couldn't precisely measure the ROI (return on investment).

I hired my first business coach when I set out to raise venture capital and realized I needed help in how to best negotiate the deals. Steve Nakisher was a friend of my senior VP of sales and marketing and an entrepreneur, psychotherapist, and businessman all rolled into one; he lived in Chicago and coached me via Skype. He helped me find a way to talk to VCs while holding my ground and in my own style. I didn't tell many people I had a coach, as I felt it would somehow send a message that I couldn't handle things on my own. Aside from budget challenges, there can also be emotional challenges to bringing on a business coach; it might feel like you're admitting that you don't know all the answers.

When I hired my public speaking coach, Bill Smartt, it was because I had a hunch that honing my presentation skills might make me stand out; at the very least it would boost my confidence. Still, I had to fight the idea that this was an extravagance. Most of my family and friends told me I didn't "need" a coach since they perceived me as someone who was good at public speaking.

Right around that time, I was reading Walter Isaacson's biography *Steve Jobs* and learned that Jobs, who is considered one of the best presenters on the planet, had worked with a public-speaking coach throughout his entire career! Even Jobs recognized that a coach could help him be better. So why should I feel embarrassed?

Working with a public-speaking coach has turned out to be one of the best career decisions I ever made. All of my coaches have remained "in my corner" long after we stopped working together and generously help me through tough times whenever I reach out. Now that I speak openly about having coaches, many of the entrepreneurs and investors I respect most tell me about *their* coaches, and other entrepreneurs, far from judging me, are asking for my coaches' names so they can up their game. One of my favorite (and funny) definitions of a coach is: someone who asks you to do things you don't want to do, so you can become the person you want to be.

## FINDING FANTASTIC ADVISORS

From the outset of Chloe + Isabel, CEO Chantel Waterbury knew that she needed flying buttresses, and specifically, the help of someone who had started a business before. At the top of her list was Millard "Mickey" Drexler, CEO of J.Crew, whom she met through an investor. He helped her with everything from creating complex organizational charts to deciding what to put on the cover of a catalogue and how to best recruit and interview job candidates. "I was shocked that someone as busy as Mickey was willing to make time for a young entrepreneur just starting out," Chantel says. "He has always made himself available if I needed his advice. One of the most valuable things has been simply being in his office and watching how he works. I've never seen anyone be able to multitask and get as much done in a thirty-minute period as he does." Sometimes Mickey relays Chantel's phone calls to someone on his staff with the expertise to answer her specific questions, and she says that is as valuable as if he took the call himself.

If you don't feel your flying buttresses are doing the job, there are some easy ways to find new ones. Good places to look are professional organizations like Levo League and the national Small Business Office's mentorship program. In my experience, creating an advisory council is a very efficient and effective way to bring in advisors and mentors, especially when you haven't yet reached the point in your business where you're ready to form an official board of advisors or can't afford to build out your staff or hire expensive consultants.

There are three main reasons to create an advisory council instead of collecting mentors or advisors on an ad hoc basis:

1. **Formalize the relationship for a win-win.** While people enjoy giving advice, they often enjoy it even more when they get credit for it. An advisory council is something that you can feature on your website and in business plans and investor pitch decks. The public recognition makes advisors feel the time they invest is being valued, and they will be more likely to make introductions for you than if you have an informal relationship.

2. **Provide value in return.** When you do this, you create a stronger two-way relationship with your advisor. In creating your advisory council, you recruit experts in their industries, and they often like to meet one another. You can provide value to them by introducing them to top people in other fields they may not have access to.

3. **Create a staging ground.** Your advisory council creates a kind of entry point for board members, investors, and even new hires. They can get to know you at a low commitment level, and you can see how they operate—whether they actually provide value, whether they answer your emails, and if they connect you to people who can help.

The first step in building an advisory council is to make a list of the types of advisors you are seeking by industry or area of expertise. You can share this list with friends, current mentors, past professors, and even your business colleagues. Sometimes you find an important advisor in an unlikely place.

Haitham, who ran Little Pim's fulfillment and warehouse, was born in Lebanon and speaks English, Arabic, and French fluently. He is raising his kids to be bilingual in French and English, so the mission of our company is close to his heart. He came out of the investment banking world and was very well connected and good at many of the parts of the business that were most challenging to me, like managing complex operational challenges and navigating the venture capital world. We began having lunch every few months to compare notes as CEOs; when I set out to raise venture capital, he was one of the first people who offered to introduce me to potential investors. He also helped me with my pitch deck (a business plan presented as a series of slides), gave good tips on negotiating, and was someone I could count on for advice about raising capital.

I helped him in return whenever I could, bringing expertise and industry insider information to him that he found valuable, referring new business to him, and getting his sales people into trade shows where we had a booth and his company did not. We enjoyed tracking each other's companies because we were on similar paths.

Many advisors will agree to work with you just to help out, or for the kind of reciprocal relationship I had with Haitham, but you can also consider a financial stipend if the person is bringing you something of great value to the company and you don't have a personal relationship to draw on. Some entrepreneurs offer stock option grants (see glossary) or just free drinks! Here is a sample email, sent by Stacey Brook to a potential advisor:

Hi John,

First of all, I finished reading *Dune* last night. This is important. We must have a conversation about this. Slightly more important at the moment, however, is this:

I was wondering if I might be able to access your advertising/ marketing expertise. I am currently on the cusp of the super busy season for my college essay advising business and a lot of my marketing channels from last year either 1. aren't giving me the return I got last year or 2. no longer exist. I was wondering if you might have time to talk, even just via G-chat (or in person!), about some potential alternative solutions.

Let me know if you might be able to help, even with a few basic suggestions. I am happy to hire you as an official consultant or pay you in dinner and cocktails. Also, I know this is super short notice, but I could meet up this weekend if you had time—and it would be nice to see you!

That said, if you don't have time for any of this, I totally understand.

Thanks so much!

Stacey

Two days later, John and Stacey sat down for drinks. John didn't become an "official advisor" to her company, but he helped Stacey identify new channels for driving traffic to her website (Facebook advertising and key word searches she hadn't thought to use) and dispensed a few tips for increasing her site's conversion rate, both of which paid off immediately in attracting new clients.

## CLOSING THE LOOP

When people help you with your business, whether it's an introduction to a potential funder or connecting you with a new client, be sure to make them feel appreciated for what they have contributed by closing the loop. This simple act of saying thank you makes you stand out from the pack, and it's just plain polite. You would be surprised how many people miss this easy (and free) opportunity to build goodwill.

I recently closed a loop with one of my advisors, Jonathan Teller, who had a direct positive impact on sales. I had asked Jonathan, who is founder and managing partner of eos Products (makers of the ubiquitous dome-shaped lip gloss ball), how he produced his television commercials. He generously walked me through the entire process in a phone call, told me how much he paid for production, how he came up with the advertising concept, and what he learned along the way. This was invaluable information. When it became clear that I could not afford to hire the producers he used, he offered to put me in touch with Jill, the head of the agency, to ask her advice.

Jill has made successful (and pricey) spots for the likes of Tropicana, Virgin Mobile, and Frito-Lay. She was gracious about taking my call and spent forty-five minutes talking through our entire commercial strategy. She shared great tips and insights about my brand positioning. Then she introduced me to a boutique (read: more affordable) New York–based production company, which was a perfect fit for my company's needs. Before speaking with Jonathan, I'd had no idea who to use for our commercials or even if we were on the right track with our campaign, and it might have taken me weeks of vetting companies to get to the right one. With two phone calls, my problem was solved. We produced a commercial within our budget and used it to drive higher conversions (more people who view our site clicking through to buy our products).

All along the way, I kept closing the loop. Once we decided to work with the company Jill recommended, I circled back to both Jonathan and Jill with thank-you emails. They both wrote back within minutes to say they were happy it had worked out.

Let's pause here a moment. Why were they helping me when it didn't advance their business in any way?

Jonathan is an advisor and friend of mine, and Jill works with him, so that part is obvious. Jill was also referring my business to a company she likes and might need a favor from in the future. But there is a less obvious reason too. Once you reach a certain level of success, helping other entrepreneurs can be one of the most gratifying parts of a CEO's day. I know hundreds of successful business owners through my involvement in EO, and, to a person, they are all giving back by either formally or informally

## LET YOUR PEERS HELP YOU ACCELERATE

My friends and colleagues in the Entrepreneurs' Organization (EO) are one of my most robust sources of support and dependable flying buttresses. My lawyer, Jonathan, had been a member of EO for over ten years when he suggested I look into joining back in 2011. I didn't meet their criterion of making over $1 million in revenues at the time, but they told me they had a program called EO Accelerator for business owners who were making north of $250,000 but hadn't yet found a path to $1 million. The program cost $1,650 for a year's worth of classes and mentoring, a far cry from the $100,000-plus of most business schools. As the mom of two young kids, the fact that I didn't have to travel anywhere or take classes on weekends was a big part of the appeal. In the course of this year-long program I went to four day-long workshops on finance, sales/marketing, people, and strategy and was assigned to a peer accountability group. The group met once a month and was made up of three other business owners and an assigned EO mentor.

One of the first things EO Accelerator emphasized is that we had to spend more time working "*on* the business, not *in* the business." That's the key message of the popular book by Michael E. Gerber, *The E-Myth*, a must-read for entrepreneurs. Gerber tells the story of a woman who starts a pie company because she loves baking but winds up hating her company and becoming exhausted and unhappy and not even making good money because she is always in the kitchen instead of working on building systems to make the company more profitable.[3] Whenever we see a peer in EO doing this, we remind her of Sarah the baker and encourage her to focus more on systems and strategy.

The EO Accelerator program gave me a group of peers, so I could share the ups and downs of Little Pim and get their help with going big. EO Accelerator also provided business school–like training in areas where I felt I still needed help, and gave me the chance to hone my skills in sales, marketing, and strategy.

My assigned EO mentor in the program, Shep Sepaniak, is a long-time EOer and led us in a funny, humble, and inspiring way that I later understood was signature EO. The types of entrepreneurs who join this organization are more interested in learning than bragging. They love build-ing businesses but also want to lift up other entrepreneurs. Shep shared the challenges he faced in his own insurance business, from cash flow issues to the changes in his field that made some of his services obsolete. This made us all feel a lot better about the struggles we were going through. When things went well at Little Pim, like when we landed a big account or were featured on *The View*, I celebrated with my Accelerator group, and when things got tough, like when I needed to fire someone on my staff, these were the first people I turned to for support and "experience shares."

As members of EO Accelerator we also had access to inspiring big-name business leaders. We were invited to select EO events where top coaches and successful entrepreneurs from around the world came to give talks, including the leadership expert Verne Harnish, the sales training guru Jack Daly, and the breakthrough and peak performance coach Gina Mollicone-Long.

If you are wondering, "How do I get in on this?," there are EO Accel-erator programs in over thirty cities in the United States and in ten coun-tries around the world. There are also other programs, like 10,000 Small Businesses, that offer entrepreneurs training and, in some cases, introduc-tions to funders. A quick Google search of your city + "entrepreneurs' organization" should give you all the local options.

## HOW TO FIND YOUR FLYING BUTTRESSES

Here are ways to find people who can be part of your entrepreneurial sup-port crew and you theirs:

- Join a professional organization for entrepreneurs like EO Accelerator, the program for up-and-coming businesses; or another entrepreneur-focused organization in your region.
- Join a shared workspace where you can socialize and trade tips (and coffee mugs) with other entrepreneurs.
- Create an accountability group with other entrepreneurs or friends pursuing ambitious professional goals. Meet once a month and share your thirty-, sixty-, and ninety-day goals

and hold one another accountable. (Download a template at juliapimsleur.com.)

- Apply to be in an accelerator. Accelerators are short-term programs in which an entrepreneur trades a usually small (under 10 percent) amount of equity for strategic help and mentoring. These accelerators are mainly for tech businesses, and you must apply and get accepted. The website Seed.db.com has a list you can search by city.
- Contact your local Small Business Office or the National Women's Business Council to find resources and other entrepreneurs.[4] The U.S. Small Business Administration works with a number of local partners to counsel, mentor, and train small businesses.

## Verne Harnish of Gazelles

As founder and CEO of Gazelles, a global executive education and coaching company, Verne Harnish has spent the past thirty years educating entrepreneurial teams. He is the founder of the Entrepreneurs' Organization and for fifteen years chaired EO's premiere CEO program, the Birthing of Giants, and WEO's Advanced Business executive program, both held at MIT. He's also the venture columnist for *Fortune* magazine.

**Is it harder for women to get to the million-dollar mark?**
Forget gender—we are talking about 94 percent of *all* companies never get to the million-dollar mark. That's why when I launched EO we set it as a benchmark: you had to get over a million to be able to get into the organization. Entrepreneurs who don't scale to that first level, it's because they are spending way too much time organizing—"Let's tweak the website" and "I want to make sure my logo looks good"—and they spend all this time and it really doesn't matter. To get to that first million, you've just got to sell. "Don't you have to have really good business cards?" No!

### If "Sell, sell, sell" is the first key, what's the second?

Focus, focus, focus. When the Airbnb guys were first asked "So, who are your customers?," they gave the typical response: "Everybody!" No. Who do you have right now? They looked at their database and saw that in New York City they had twenty customers. They went to New York and they met with these customers and figured out that the photos they were taking themselves and uploading were terrible, and they didn't know how to write a description of the place. So they hired professionals to take the photos and copywriters to produce the descriptions, and that made all the difference once they got those two things right. They didn't say, "Let's go try to conquer twenty-seven cities at the same time."

### Any tips for staying focused?

One hour a week, even if it's just with yourself, you should have a one-hour strategy meeting to say, "Who already has been where I'm about to go?" And your job is to go find them and get them to help you.

### So few women-run businesses are making over a million in revenue. Why the gap?

A woman I know was disappointed that she was one of only seven women in the first MIT program. She started an EO chapter in San Francisco to fix it and came back and told us some things she'd learned: Women tend to be older when they start a business. If they already have children or are contemplating children, then they may rank them much higher on the priority list than men do. Traditionally men have not minded being away from home as much. To succeed you need to be spending 80 percent of your week outside the office, out selling.

### What else do we need to do differently?

I met with a woman who built a hundred-million-dollar company. She launched a new business and said, "I think we can do $1.8 million in three years." I told her, "Look, no one is going to pay attention if you don't paint a picture that it's going to a hundred million. And you can paint that picture, because you've done it before." She nodded, but then she said, "I think women don't or can't BS like men can!"

***Is there a point at which fundraising is most important?***

After you hit a million in revenues. Because by then you probably figured out what you really are good at and what the business model looks like. Hitting a million means that you passed a test, that you actually have something that enough people want, and that you have clawed your way there. You probably have some entrepreneurial chops and you are in the top 6 percent. At the end of the day, investors are investing in the idea and the people.

# 5

# TURN MOXIE INTO MONEY

I met Kelly in Las Vegas at a trade show for baby and young children's products. Kelly was just launching her first business and she had come to scout for products for her baby store in Charlotte, North Carolina. She had done her research and studied what made similar shops successful in cities nearby. Her two children were now grown, and she was ready to create the business she had dreamed about for years. Her face lit up as she told me about her boutique, which would sell upscale products for newborns. I thought it sounded like it had real potential. "How are you going to finance this?" I asked.

Kelly paused as if this was not a question she had thought much about, and then answered, "I'm drawing on my savings. If everything goes smoothly, I should have enough to last me six months." Then her voice got very quiet and she added, with a concerned look, "And if not, I guess I can always dip into my retirement, though that wouldn't be good."

My heart sank as I imagined all the cash she was going to lay out to buy products, decorate, purchase insurance, and get up and running, and the likelihood that she would reach the end of her financial tether all too soon. I decided to tell it to her straight: "Kelly, chances are high that something *will* go wrong. Something always does with a new business. To start a business you really need enough working capital to last you a whole year, and preferably eighteen months. That gives you a longer runway to take off."

I told her about what happened to me, how within my first two years, our key distributor went bankrupt and took $120,000 of our money with him, about the accounts that didn't pay for months, and about the day our office ceiling literally fell in. We heard some odd drips from the ceiling and then a loud crash as a four-foot strip of tin fell onto our desks. No one was hurt, thankfully, but we had to evacuate immediately and find new offices within a week.

The kind of boutique Kelly was setting up is what is known as a "lifestyle business." This is a business that allows its owners to work while supporting a lifestyle they enjoy. However, lifestyle businesses rarely attract investors, as they do not have the potential to turn into high-revenue-generating, fast-growing businesses that have a big payout. I asked Kelly if she had considered raising money from friends and family. We discussed how, in addition to the store, she could build a website and sell her carefully curated products 24/7, at first in neighboring cities and eventually—Why not?—all across the country. I knew Kelly could turn this into a much bigger opportunity than just a lifestyle business if she had not only the moxie but a plan for converting it into cash.

"I don't know if I would be comfortable asking other people to put money in," she replied. "What if it doesn't work out and I lose their savings?"

"You don't have to protect the investors," I pointed out. "It's their money and their responsibility. They will invest only if they think your business has a chance of succeeding." I explained that there are laws surrounding investments, most notably the Securities and Exchange Commission (SEC) regulation that any investors must be accredited and have enough disposable income to ensure that what they are putting into your company is not what they plan to retire on.[1] Accredited investors usually have a portfolio of investments that includes some longer-term, riskier bets, and investing in Kelly's company would fall in that category.

The more we talked about it, the more Kelly warmed up to the idea of building something bigger and more fundable, and she started coming up with people in her social circles she felt she could ask for a small investment and who could help her with advice and contacts. She left promising she would give fundraising serious consideration. She planned to start by having lunch with a friend who had raised money for his business to see if he would make some initial introductions.

Kelly's hesitation around fundraising is a widespread reaction among women entrepreneurs. But *not* raising capital can have significant long-term implications. Women-run businesses make 27 percent of the revenues of those run by men, and this is at least in part because they start out with much less capital than their male counterparts, who get up to six times more.[2] I asked Jonathan Teller, founder of eos Products, who is also one of my advisors and does angel investing, about the differences between how men and women seek investment for their new companies. He said he and other angels are skeptical of an entrepreneur who hasn't raised any money. Angel investors have this attitude: "If you don't feel confident enough to go to your own circles for funding, why should anyone outside your immediate friends and family invest?" By not asking, women can get caught in a "Don't ask, don't get" cycle that perpetuates itself and makes later fundraising even harder.

It's also a systemic problem. According to the National Women's Business Council, men have an easier time getting loans and tend to be more bullish about raising capital even when they are just at the back-of-the-napkin phase. And these gaps persist past the start-up phase. Studies show that women-owned firms are less likely to take in outside financing, including loans, angel investments, and venture capital, in the course of the company's life. There is a direct correlation between the amount of capital a business has and its chances of earning high revenues.[3] No wonder 97 percent of women-run companies have no employees and revenues of less than $250,000 per year. But it doesn't have to be that way.

So why are women like Kelly not asking for the capital they need? I believe there are four reasons:

1. They don't know how much of a disadvantage it will be not to have it.
2. They are afraid they might fail and disappoint their investors.
3. They don't know how or where to raise funds. They don't have the right personal or professional networks to gain access to capital.
4. They are not trained in how to find and lock in investors. They don't know which types of funding instruments to use or how to build a compelling narrative about their company. So even if they get the meeting, they don't get the investment. In the meantime, guys are calling up their buddies and saying, "Dude, I just started a company. You in for $25K?"

But it's like what they say on the Harvard undergraduate admissions tour: "The only way you can guarantee you won't get into Harvard is not to apply." I'm going to teach you how to do the equivalent of filling out that Ivy League application. With the right plan and the right funding, you really can get the capital you need to expand your business.

## THE FOUR KEY QUESTIONS TO ASK BEFORE RAISING CAPITAL

Once you have determined that you have a business that offers a fundable, preferably highly scalable opportunity (see the exercises at the end of the book if you still aren't sure), there are four questions that can guide you in deciding which kind of capital is right for your company:

1.   What forms of capital should I consider?
2.   When is it the right time to raise money?
3.   Where do I learn the fundraising dance?
4.   How much equity and control will I have to give up?

Let's take these one at a time.

## 1. WHAT FORMS OF CAPITAL SHOULD I CONSIDER?

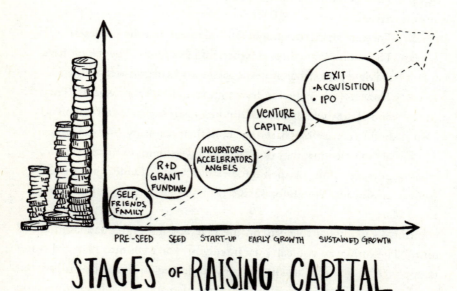

STAGES of RAISING CAPITAL

This chart shows the stages in which people usually raise each type of capital. Most businesses raise capital in their first one to three years of existence. When companies have revenues in the $800,000 to $1.5 million range, that is the stage when they typically start seeking venture capital. A seed round is usually for friends and family or angels, though in the past few years a handful of VCs have started investing at the seed stage and the lines are blurry between seed and angel. A Series A round can be made up of all angels, or angels and VCs. The Series B and C (and so on) are usually for VCs but can still be made up of angels, either the same ones who invested in Series A or new investors. If you are wondering which kind of capital investment is right for you at the stage you are at with your business, here is a quick breakdown.

## Crowdfunding

There are actually two types of crowdfunding: "rewards-based" and "equity." You have probably already had a friend hit you up for rewards-based funding. Sites like Kickstarter and Indiegogo allow you to invite people to essentially pre-buy your company's products by spending relatively small amounts (usually in the $25- to $1,000-per-person range). These campaigns work only with companies that are actually selling a product; if you are launching a tech start-up and offering a free service, for example, you won't be eligible. Note that no one opens their computer and says, "I want to invest today." You'll need to wow people with your product and pitch (usually via a short video) about why they should invest, plus tap into your own network to write the first checks.

Equity crowdfunding is what it sounds like: people are actually buying stock (equity) in your company. As I write this book, selling equity online (selling shares in your company) is not approved by the SEC unless it's to an accredited investor, and most crowdfunding sites do not have a very robust way of determining if the investors are accredited; they typically allow people to self-qualify as accredited investors with a few clicks and do very little verifying, if any. (As a caveat, the ultimate responsibility for ensuring an investor is an accredited investor lies with the company taking the money.)

Entrepreneurs use crowdfunding to test an idea or launch a new product (one of the most famous early examples is the Pebble Smartwatch, which raised over $10 million on Kickstarter) or finance a new line of products within their business. At Little Pim we did a Kickstarter campaign that raised $13,000 to make a new holiday eBook featuring our panda character traveling around the world. Our rewards included having drawings of your children in the book, a high-quality printed coffee-table version, and me reading the book to your child via Skype. You can raise any amount you want through crowdfunding, but the average is in the $10,000 to $80,000 range.

Not all businesses lend themselves to crowdfunding, but if yours qualifies, there are three big advantages to raising initial monies this way. First, it may generate cash relatively quickly that you can use to expand your company. (I say "may" because not all campaigns are successful.) Second, you do not have to sell shares in your company. You keep total control of your company whether you raise $20,000 or $20 million. Third, if you have a business selling directly to consumers, you are essentially raising money from your future customers and building your customer list along with getting the cash. This can be great data to have to wow a future investor, whether angel or VC.

Each crowdfunding site provides abundant tips on how to run a successful campaign and tap into your existing networks, which you will need to mobilize in order to meet your goal. Women are particularly good at crowdfunding, it turns out, because this platform draws heavily on social media, where women outnumber men and usually maintain several active networks on Facebook, Pinterest, Twitter, and LinkedIn. Debbie Sterling, the founder of GoldieBlox, an engineering toy for girls, raised $285,000 on Kickstarter, which allowed her to place her first order of five thousand units of her product. She then went on to raise angel and venture capital and told the story of her successful crowdfunding campaign to potential investors as proof of interest and market validation.

There are downsides to crowdfunding. First, raising money this way is almost as time-consuming as raising traditional seed money or money from friends and family (you should allow two to six months, from planning to the end of a crowdfunding campaign) but does not usually bring in as much capital. Second, the crowdfunding investors usually aren't repeat investors and are less likely to have additional funds for subsequent cash needs. Third, crowdfunding does not give you the kind of industry validation you get from raising angel or venture capital; this is because due diligence is not required. (Due diligence is when potential investors complete background checks and put the company through its paces to ensure the financials are in order and the projections stand up to pressure testing.) The people who pre-buy items online are not considered savvy investors, so they don't give the company the stamp of approval that you get with traditional investors.

Overall, though, crowdfunding is one of the more expeditious ways to raise funds, and women have fewer barriers to entry than they do when raising other kinds of capital. To be successful, you need to be able to make a compelling video, offer tempting rewards, and get ready to tap all your friends (and their friends) via email and social media. You can use general crowdfunding sites like Kickstarter and Indiegogo or women-specific sites like Plum Alley and Circle Up, often first stops for women investors who want to support women entrepreneurs. Just be sure to read the fine print because some sites let you keep the money only if you raise your entire goal.

## Deborah Jackson of Plum Alley

After twenty-one years on Wall Street, Deborah Jackson decided that women needed more opportunities to succeed and more access to capital. In 2010 she started a newsletter about women and technology, and got plugged into the burgeoning start-up scene in New York City, where she saw a deficiency of funds for women's ideas and their companies. This experience affirmed a need to support women in reaching their dreams and having impact in the world. Plum Alley, a funding platform for women's projects and companies, was founded in response to this need. Most campaigns look to raise $25,000, though there's no limit to how much you can ask for. Already women have pursued campaigns to raise millions of dollars.

### Which types of companies or projects are most suitable for funding?

We see all types of projects and companies, from do-good-in-the-world projects, creative projects, product and company launches, and more. Many projects will be created to solve problems and needs that are unique to women. Our Plum Alley audience is comprised of enthused individuals who are not only advocates of women entrepreneurship but can directly relate with many of the causes and projects that will be raising capital on our site.

For instance, we had one project with a bottled-water company that delivered necessary nutrients for women. The founder wanted to introduce a new flavor—so she did a campaign where people pre-ordered her product. By going for pre-orders of her new product, she knew there was demand and she was able to get the necessary money to go to production of that new flavor. If you are in an existing company and you want to test-market a new product line or a new feature, you can very easily do that. Another campaign creator was a woman who had an established eco-friendly cleaning product company and wanted to introduce a mobile app. She went to her existing customer base and said, "Okay, you like what I do. Help me raise money so I can build a mobile app for you." Her customer base funded it. Keep in mind, 80 percent of the money raised will come from people you know with a dedicated and compelling campaign.

It's really important which company and platform you associate with, especially if your customer is a woman. Sites like Kickstarter attract a certain demographic—mostly younger men. If you have a company that offers a product for women, and you want to reach your target customer, then Plum Alley is the best bet for you as our audience is 78 percent female. Women will also benefit from being in a place that champions women entrepreneurs and provides a community to help your company.

### Is crowdfunding a good precursor to other types of fundraising, or are more traditional routes, like friends and family, more important?

It is becoming more common that venture capitalists say, "Have you done a crowdfunding campaign?" They know the value of test-marketing a product and gaining traction in an early-stage company. With a successful funding campaign, a founder can easily demonstrate the attributes that are necessary to run a start-up: asking for money with an organized campaign and proper marketing to sell your concept. You have to tell your story, and it requires a certain amount of confidence. I see crowdfunding as the very first step before you reach out to a "friends and family" round or even before an angel or venture round. If you can raise half a million dollars of pre-orders for a product without giving away any equity, you should do that.

## Loans and Grants

There are traditional ways to finance your business, such as small business loans you can access through a bank, a local small business office, or peer lending sites like Prosper. You can also try to get a line of credit to help with cash flow by going to a local bank and showing your income history. In certain sectors, like education and biotech, you may also be able to apply for research grants to help pay for the development of your idea. There are always new financing initiatives popping up at the local and national levels. You can learn about the latest opportunities by reading *Entrepreneur, Inc.*, and other business publications; checking the websites for the National Women's Business Council or the U.S. Small Business Administration; and asking fellow entrepreneurs who have raised funds. The SBA will even guarantee loans for small businesses that meet their criteria.

If you are considering loans, they tend to be in the $50,000 to $500,000 range. Many women access their first capital this way, though loans can be harder to get for first-time business owners, as you don't yet have any credit history. Women are 15 to 20 percent less likely to get a loan than their male counterparts, according to research by the National Women's Business Council, but given that a loan allows you to retain more control of your company than equity financing (people buying shares of your company), it's worth exploring if you qualify.[4] If you are a member of a minority population (women count) or are working in an area that has experienced economic distress, you may be eligible for a loan/investment from a CDFI (Community Development Financial Institution); the mission of a CDFI is to invest and make loans in underserved communities.

The best way to go after a loan is to show up in person at a bank near your business and create a relationship with a bank officer. It also helps if you can get an introduction from a business person in your community who is already banking with that institution or if you have done your personal banking there. Be sure to ask the banker who from your company will need to sign if you do qualify for a loan, because if you already have angel investors and you own less than 50 percent of the company, you may need signatures and personal tax documents from your investors. You also may be asked to put up your home or other personal assets to guarantee the loan, which gives many entrepreneurs pause and makes asking friends and family or angels seem like a better option.

## Friends and Family

Friends and family are usually the first stop in equity fundraising. Many people begin here because this gets you started on a path to larger raises. Friends and family are people who are willing to take a chance on you and your business because they trust you. Sometimes this group is also referred to as "friends, family, and fools" because they usually don't put the company through the kind of paces that later investors do. They tend to write checks in the $10,000 to $50,000 range, and they are really investing in you. A typical amount to raise through friends and family is $300,000 to $500,000. Many CEOs use convertible debt agreements with their friends and family investors, which allow people to invest before there is a first big official investment round; their investment then converts to stock when the round takes place. Talk with your lawyer about the different options for taking in capital and your company's legal structure, and see the glossary for more information.

## Angel Investors

Angel investors are the next stop for growth capital, and friends and family can ultimately get rolled up into the angel round (the difference between the two is sometimes more semantics). Close to 90 percent of the money invested in early-stage businesses each year comes from angels, who invest a collective $25 billion per year in companies. Angel investment is a common way for start-ups to bridge the gap between the relatively small dollars they raise from friends and family and a larger venture capital round when their revenues or other key performance indicators (see glossary) can attract the bigger dollar investments. Often VCs want to see evidence of significant traction before they invest, such as $1 million in revenues or one million users, but angels are usually less stringent about your having already met these milestones. Angels may care what kind of a corporation you have for their tax filings and may be more comfortable investing if you have an LLC or C-Corp rather than an S-Corp.

A good place to start your research is a site like Crunchbase, where you can see who funded your competitors. AngelList.com has a robust database of active angels who are accredited investors. Sites where you can list your company for angel investors to consider include FundersClub and MicroVentures. The investors looking for deals on these sites are what the SEC calls "qualified investors," which, as I mentioned previously, are people who have significant disposable income and will not end up on welfare even if the investment goes south.

You can search these sites by market, to see what other companies in your space are raising capital, and by location, to find angels near you (most angels prefer to invest locally). There are an increasing number of women angel investors (the number jumped from 19 percent in 2013 to 26 percent in 2014),[5] and research shows that angel investor groups with a high number of women devote a higher percentage of their dollars to women-owned firms. You can contact angels directly via some of the sites mentioned here, but it's preferable to get referred by a mutual contact, so first go over to LinkedIn to see if you know anyone in common. While having access to so many potential investors is great, you can also easily get lost among the thousands of companies seeking their attention. Angels typically invest smaller amounts than VCs do (angel investments range from $15,000 to $500,000) in a handful of companies.

There are actually two types of angel investors: those who invest in just a few companies and typically in people they know (sometimes called "casual angels") and professional angels. To find out what kind of angel someone is, you can ask, "How many checks have you written in the past twelve months?" and "What was the average size?" If they haven't made more than two or three investments, they are a casual angel, which might mean they may make you jump through fewer hoops. But it also may mean they are less used to writing checks, so it could take longer to seal the deal.

Professional angels have requirements that look a bit more like those of VCs. They will want to perform due diligence on your company, and in this process they will ask to see, among other things, every contract with your key accounts, as well as a detailed financial model of how your business works. Investors call this asking you to "open your kimono." (No comment!) Professional angels, like VCs, take a portfolio approach to investing, which means they put money into several companies in specific sectors they follow, like education or consumer retail. The portfolio approach also means they expect some of their investments to do really well, some to come out just average, and some to fail. You can find the professional angels pooling their funds in angel investor groups in all major cities, and they often have sessions for which you can apply to come pitch them all at once. If you are not accepted to pitch or are not the right fit for an angel investor group, don't worry. Close to 90 percent of angels are not affiliated with any of these groups. The best way to find them is to do extensive online searches and network like crazy.

With angels it is possible to get from an introduction to a yes in three to five months, which would be considered a fast sprint in the venture capital world. Related to angel groups are "family offices," investing entities that act like angels except they are investing the funds of one or more wealthy individuals or families. They are usually a little more off the radar than angel groups and fund people referred by a member of the family.

Venture capitalists tend to write bigger checks than angels, typically between $500,000 and $50 million. Venture capitalists invested $48.3 billion in 4,356 deals in 2014, and that number is expected to keep rising.[6] It used to be that VCs would invest only when a company had proof of concept (their product had been tested and met the approval of hundreds or thousands of customers) and significant initial revenues ($1 million plus), but since 2010 more VCs have started investing at the seed stage, or much earlier than they previously did. These seed investments are typically smaller (in the $200,000 to $1 million range) and are a way for VCs to get involved earlier so they don't miss out on owning a stake in one of the ultimate big winners. Most VCs who do not fund at the seed stage will not consider making investments under $3 million. It's simply not worth their time when they can spend the same internal resources on a $10 million or $25 million investment. Be sure to do your research, because what VCs put out in the public domain (e.g., via their websites) can be stale in terms of describing what size checks they are writing. Be sure to track what they have done through Crunchbase and other sites, and talk to CEOs who have received investments from them to see how they really operate.

In short, you should consider raising venture capital if you meet these criteria:

- Your company is going after a market worth at least $1 billion.
- You plan on exiting (selling your company or doing an initial public offering) within five to seven years and doing so in a way that generates a 5-times to 10-times return.
- Your company is growing fast (revenues are doubling year over year, or close to it).
- You are focused on increasing your company's value and may even forgo profitability for higher revenues (e.g., your sales are growing quickly even if you are having to add more staff and spend more on marketing to get there).
- You feel ready to work with VCs to take the company big, whatever that takes. This could include firing current staff, needing to find new strategic partners, or reducing your cost of goods.
- You are willing to bring new investors on your board from the venture capital institution. These people could potentially determine at some point that you are not the right person to lead the company. In that case, you would retain your ownership level at the time of transition but not be at the helm.

When you find the right venture capital firm, it can be a true partner that brings contacts and resources to the table and helps you ramp up quickly. With the cash infusion, you'll be able to spend more on staff, marketing, operations, and product development. That's the good news. The downside is that the VCs usually get one or two board seats and 25 to

30 percent ownership. Once you take venture capital money, the pressure is on to grow aggressively and scale up quickly. You'll need to think constantly about how you are positioning the company for an exit—whether you are on track with your revenue projections and when you will sell the company, either to a strategic partner or a private equity firm or, in a handful of cases, have an initial public offering. If you are looking to build a business you will be running yourself for decades or passing down to family members, venture capital is not the way to go.

If you really can't bear the idea of going out to look for investors on your own, consider hiring a company that will make introductions (private bankers or boutique fundraising advisors). There are scores of middlemen waiting for your phone call or email to help you find investors. The problem here is that these companies or individuals usually want a retainer (to the tune of tens of thousands of dollars) plus 5 to 7 percent of the invested amount. And most angels and VCs think if you have to use one of these firms, then maybe you aren't a go-getter CEO. So in my humble opinion, you are better off fundraising yourself, with the help of your advisors, friends, and Google.

## Which Is Right for You?

Each type of capital has different timelines and requirements. Raising angel money is more of a sprint (three to six months, once you have your pitch down and deck in place, depending on how much money you are looking for), while raising venture capital is a marathon. According to a Harvard Business School study, it takes an average of twenty-one months for entrepreneurs to secure venture capital funding, though most of the CEOs I know did it in under fifteen months, so it really depends on the CEO, her track record and network, and the opportunity.[7] There are more roads that lead to finding angels, and angels tend to decide more quickly than VCs, who often need to get buy-in from multiple partners before they invest.

Angels are investing in part to have the experience of accompanying an entrepreneur on a journey of building a business, so the more you can convey your passion and willingness to work hard and be transparent about your progress and your setbacks, the more enticing you will be. You also want them to see that you are coachable and will be open to their suggestions and feedback. But at the end of the day, the main thing you need to convey is how they will be able to make a return on their investment, so it's important to practice, practice, and practice your pitch so that you have a clear and concise description of where the company is going and how you plan to take it there.

## Gigi Lee Chang of Plum Organics

COURTESY OF GIGI LEE CHANG

Gigi Lee Chang is the cofounder and former CEO of Plum Organics, one of the top makers of organic baby food, with nationwide distribution in stores like Whole Foods and Target. Entrepreneurship is in her blood; her parents ran a sports-equipment company in China. In 2008 Plum Organics was sold to the Nest Collective. Gigi is a good example of a woman who knew when it was time to sell. She was more recently the CEO of the national nonprofit Healthy Child Healthy World.

*In 2008 you left the role of CEO at Plum Organics and stepped away from the day-to-day. How did that happen?*

I needed a break. You have to think about your own well-being, your own family. I started my company when my son was nine months old. When I joined forces with the operating company, we were over a million dollars. I stepped away from it, and then they took it from a million to the exit [a sale to Campbell's Soup Company]. I remained involved in terms of our marketing outreach, but it was the brand that carried it through.

*How did you finance your company initially?*

I was able to self-fund. But it always took more capital than we anticipated. At the end of the day, we ended up putting in probably about three times more than we thought at the beginning. I had never done a start-up before. From starting to launch was about eight months, and then from being in the market to when we got our first shot at financing was about fifteen months.

***Tell me about your first round of angel investment.***

I was fortunate in that it was a family office—just one family. When you are in a position of looking for capital, you feel like you are really lucky if they are giving you their time. But at a certain point in the process I came to the realization that they are getting something out of this: the opportunity for their capital to grow and to be part of something really exciting. You need to say, "What kind of investor am I looking for?" It's okay to walk away from somebody even if they seem right on paper. If it just doesn't feel right, you should trust that intuition. When in doubt, ask the investor for references from the other companies they funded. As much as they are doing due diligence on you, it's important for you to do due diligence on potential funders.

***Do you have any other tips about investing?***

Once you raise money, you are on the path where in a certain window of time there is an expectation that the company will be sold. Even with "mission-aligned" investors, they aren't giving you money out of the goodness of their heart. They are expecting a return on it.

## Warning: Rock Dudes Ahead

Venture capital is the toughest kind of money to raise for every entrepreneur, regardless of gender. Angels invest in one out of every ten businesses they vet; VCs invest in one out of a hundred.[8] So you are ten times more likely to be successful raising angel money than venture capital.[9] Women have an even steeper hill to climb. Only 4 to 7 percent of venture capital investment in the United States goes to women-run companies, depending on which studies you read. It climbs to 12 percent if you include companies with women on the senior leadership team, but these are still very small numbers.

VCs are notorious for being a mostly white, mostly all boys' club. When my husband and our two young boys went on a camping trip one summer and had to tough it out against the elements, they started jokingly calling themselves the "Rock Dudes," and the name stuck. I decided their little guys' club was harmless and sort of funny. Now when they are having all-boys time, like when I am on a business trip, that's how they refer to themselves. I can't help but think VCs are the Rock Dudes of the investment world. They are having a good time, are making killer profits, and are not eager to let anyone else into their club.

That can make it daunting to try to break in as a female entrepreneur or a female investor. Only 6 percent of venture capital partners are women, and the number of women in venture capital has been declining, not increasing, though many women in that sector are working hard to change that.[10] If you look at any venture capital firm's website, you will see that while they may have women on staff, few of them are decision makers. On the Forbes Midas list of the top one hundred VCs—the big-money decision makers—the grand total of women was four in 2014. Not surprisingly, firms that have a female partner are twice as likely to invest in companies with a woman on the executive team. Venture capital firms with women in decision-making positions are three times more likely to invest in companies with a female CEO.[11]

There are also plenty of infuriating stories about women who receive unwanted advances from potential investors or who are treated with condescension or outright hostility. But we can't let those stories hold us back. There are bad actors in all sectors, not just the fundraising world. And there are a whole lot of good guys too. I have many men friends in the angel and venture capital world who are passionate about seeing more women at the table. You just need to make sure to find the good ones. By talking to other CEOs who have raised money and doing a little Internet research on sites like TheFunded.com, it's not hard to sort out the toads from the team players.

Some women VCs are actually leaving the Rock Dudes' boardrooms to start their own funds, in part because they are tired of the dude culture and, in some cases, because they have an explicit mission of supporting women entrepreneurs. Golden Seeds, a collective of investors that has chapters in six major U.S. cities (and is the backer of Little Pim), has an angel group and manages two funds through which its investors contribute venture capital to women-led companies. They are the largest of the women-focused funds and invest only in companies with at least one female founder. Astia, an investing group that has moved from supporting women entrepreneurs through a training model to securing them funding with its own angel group, also plans to raise a fund, as does Springboard. There are new investment groups popping up all the time: California-based Cowboy Ventures, led by Aileen Lee; Aspect Ventures, cofounded by Jennifer Fonstad and Theresia Gouw; Rivet Ventures, with cofounders Shadi Meharein, Rebeca Hwang, and Christina A. Brodbeck; Future Perfect Ventures, founded by Jalak Jobanputra; and Female Founders Fund, founded by Anu Duggal. Longer standing female-founded and -run funds that are active and well known include Illuminate Ventures (Cindy Padnos) and Forerunner Ventures (Kirsten Green). However, the good news is mitigated because these women-run funds represent a tiny slice of the billions of dollars VCs invest each year.

Women who made it into the Rock Dudes' club are trying to change that culture from within. In the next decade, VCs will look very different, and I do believe they will eventually reflect the diversity in American society. Studies show that when a minority group gets up to 30 percent representation in any majority group, issues of discrimination start to subside. However, we are still a long way from 30 percent, so don't wait for that change to go raise the funds you need for your business! You might be pitching to rooms full of men in the near term, but you can absolutely get funded if you are good at presenting your vision, have your limiting beliefs in check, and know your business inside and out. At the end of the day, VCs are laser-focused on returns, and if women can generate them, men will invest.

## What Is Your Company Worth, and Who Gets to Decide?

*Valuation* is what the investor and you agree the company is worth at the time of the investment. As a ballpark, most tech start-ups are valued between $2 and 4 million.[12] But setting valuation is more an art than a science. The best way to determine your valuation is to talk to fellow CEOs about how they set theirs, look at comparable companies in your space and what they are worth, and track any sales of companies in your space. (If a company in your space is earning high revenues or was recently acquired for a big number, that will help you set your valuation higher.) Setting the valuation also requires good old-fashioned negotiating skills. The valuation of your company is extremely important because it will determine how much ownership you have after the investment. If your company is deemed to be worth—or valued at—$3 million and someone is putting in $500,000, he or she will own 16 percent of your company. If the company is worth $5 million, that same $500,000 will get the investor just 10 percent ownership.

My lead investor, Marion, came on in February 2007 at a fairly modest valuation of only about a quarter-million "pre-money" (the value of the company before the investor adds his or her investment to it). But in April 2007, I was able to begin to raise the next round from new investors at a $3 million pre-money valuation, which was about ten times the company's valuation just a few months earlier. So while Marion's initial deal wasn't ideal for me in theory, she made one genuinely life-changing contribution: together we asked for a $3 million valuation from the new angel investors just a few months later, and the next $40,000 she and her husband invested was at that higher valuation. In working with Marion, I had to give up a good chunk of my company, but I gained a terrific champion for Little Pim and credibility from having raised angel money. It wasn't an amazing deal, and I struggled with having to give up the equity, but I was eager to get my first money in so I could find bigger investors, and having Marion enabled me to do that. I still owned over 40 percent of my company; and I wanted to have a smaller piece of a bigger pie rather than a huge slice of a mini pizza.

My first big round of fundraising, the seed round, was largely made up of friends and family and introductions made by existing investors. I raised $1 million largely through passion, having strong and credible projections, and being able to compare my business's potential earnings to successful businesses in my space, like Rosetta Stone. I kept investors informed with quarterly updates, office visits, and sample products sent to their families. We had double-digit growth year after year, so everyone was relatively happy, even if we didn't exactly hit the ambitious revenue projections we had initially set forth. I learned from other CEOs that in your first few years, investors realize you may have overshot your projections a little (and sometimes a lot), but as long as the company is growing and the value is going up, most of them will take the long view and continue to rally around the company. It's worth noting that, as a rule of thumb, investors typically expect about half the growth and double the expenses that entrepreneurs project! At the early stage, the only sure thing about financial projections is that they are bound to be wrong.

Many of my angels did rally and reinvested when we went back for more capital in subsequent rounds. An investor who believes in you and is following the story of your company through the reports you send out and interactions you have throughout the year (calls, one-on-one meetings) has a higher chance of reinvesting when you need more capital. Angels usually have a pro-rata right, which means they have the right to reinvest as part of their initial investment. (You are obliged to make room for their money in each subsequent round.) They also have incentive to put more money in because each time you bring in new investors their share gets diluted. By investing in new rounds, they can keep their ownership level at the same amount. By the end of my fourth year in business I had raised a total of $2.5 million from about twenty-five investors, which funded the six-videos series in eleven languages, national marketing campaigns, and the hiring of two highly experienced new staff, one in sales and one in finance.

## Whose Money Is Being Invested?

When considering angel or venture capital, the first crucial thing to understand is that angels invest their own money, while VCs invest someone else's. The VCs raise rounds of capital from limited partners (LPs; typically large institutions like college endowments, city or state pension funds, and funds-of-funds), and they need to keep those investors happy. Those VCs have to report back to their LPs regularly, and their funds have to perform if they are to have any hope of raising the next round of financing to invest in a new slate of businesses.

Angels can have many motivations in addition to financial ones, such as staying current in a space, giving back to the next generation of entrepreneurs, and making social connections, while VCs have only one goal: to make a return for their investors, preferably within the span of a few years. When you raise money from VCs you have essentially signed up for *their* business model. In their model the only way for them to get their money back out of your company is for you to scale up quickly and get ready to sell within five to seven years. They will not be understanding or sympathetic if you miss your projections for whatever reason, as this only delays their return and makes their LPs worry that they bet on the wrong horse. It's high dollars, high pressure, and high stakes for everyone involved.

Angel and venture are expensive forms of capital because it's very time-consuming to go after them. It's common for a company's revenues to be negatively impacted in the year the CEO is out raising capital, so you have to prepare for that both financially and psychologically. Make sure you have enough cash flow to take you through the entire raise period, even if it takes longer than you expected.

Keep in mind that while these pitch meetings can also be incredibly stressful, over time you will learn your own personal strategies for managing them. In my most recent capital raise, the Series C round, I met with an investor I had been cultivating for months. I believed he was all set to invest $50,000 in Little Pim, and this was to be the lunch where we made it official. As he sat down across from me, he smiled in a sort of embarrassed way and said, "Thank you so much for meeting with me, even though I decided I won't be making an investment in Little Pim right now."

For a moment I froze. He had shown no signs of reluctance, and his decision threw me for a major loop. A few years ago I might have given up then and there. Instead I made a split-second decision to simply ignore the no. I didn't even acknowledge what he'd said but just stayed positive and kept the conversation going.

"You've given me such helpful financial advice," I said and began updating him on new developments in the company and some of our exciting new partnerships. He said that even though he wasn't investing, he wanted to keep helping with the finances and making introductions for us. After we talked about the company and were moving on to espresso, I took a deep breath and said we were growing fast and were really looking for "smart money" now—investors who also offered just the kind of helpful advice and great connections he possessed. "And that," I said, "is why I want to ask you to become one of the inner-circle investors and to come in for $50,000."

"You drive a hard bargain," he responded. "Okay, let's do this."

In the course of that lunch, the no became a yes. I had worked with enough investors to realize that a no is often a "convince me a little more." These are skills that come with many conversations, good listening, and putting limiting beliefs like "He probably isn't investing because he thinks my company doesn't have big potential" in mini-storage.

## 2. WHEN IS IT THE RIGHT TIME TO RAISE MONEY?

Raising money isn't right for every person or every business. The vast majority of businesses do not raise angel or venture capital; many are able to get loans, or tap into their customer base and get them to pre-pay for products, or fund growth off revenues. But if you have solid reasons to believe there is a bigger opportunity you could go after if you had more money for professional staff, better marketing, or improved technology, then raising funds is likely the way to go. You need to see not just modest increased revenues but a truly big opportunity you want to go after—and you have to be able to tell the story of how the new capital will get you there. You do not need to have high current revenues to raise angel money ($100,000–$300,000 is considered good early traction), but if you are a first-time entrepreneur it's best to have already proven the value of your company in some way before you set out to raise venture capital, through either revenue or growth. This can mean having reached about $1 million in revenues, having secured valuable patents or intellectual property (I.P.), or having one million eyeballs looking at your site.

If you have the kind of business where you can get to positive cash flow after raising friends-and-family or angel money, you may opt to build more slowly and reinvest your profits instead of raising additional capital. You can also negotiate a strategic partnership (see glossary) with a vendor or partner that saves you significant cash because they are giving you favorable terms or agreeing to get paid on a longer timetable. Then you can use the cash in your business. That is likely a better and easier solution than raising funds. But those situations are fairly rare. If you are like most entrepreneurs, you need access to additional capital to make investments in inventory, sales, and marketing before you can take your business to scale. As Verne Harnish puts so delicately in his book *Scaling Up*, a must read for every entrepreneur, "Growth sucks cash."[13] Here is the rub: not having cash will actually hamper your growth. While there certainly are businesses that use their annual profits to finance growth and thereby avoid raising money, they are in the minority. The majority of entrepreneurs need capital to take their business to the next level. That's why it's called *growth capital*.

With Little Pim, I was building a brand and competing for customers and "share of wallet" (how much consumers spend on a certain kind of product or service) with the likes of Disney, Nickelodeon, and Fisher Price. To go big, I had to have a substantial marketing budget and professional staff who knew how to deploy it. I also had to earn a salary to help support my family, even if I was paying myself below market rate for a CEO.

What's more, I felt certain there would be a big payout for anyone who invested in me and my company, so raising funds would be giving more people the opportunity to come along for the future win. When I was a full-time fundraiser a family friend once told me with barely concealed disdain, "I really couldn't do what you do: ask people for money all day." Like I was selling babies on the corner! Here's one of my secrets to success: I really have never thought I was "asking people for money." I was showing them in my pitch deck what I saw in my head—what Little Pim would look like when it was operating at scale in a few years' time. I also followed a rule I had learned while I was a nonprofit fundraiser: never ask for money until you are 90 percent sure they will say yes. If you are going into a meeting anxious about asking, then likely you have not yet spent enough time helping them understand your organization and why it's a good investment. "No" often simply means, "I don't *know* enough yet."

## A FUNDRAISING CASE STUDY: MILKMADE

Diana Hardeman, creator of MilkMade Ice Cream, a New York–based "ice cream of the month club," spent four years making custom ice-cream flavors and having them hand-delivered to her customers before she decided it was time to get bigger and raise capital to do so. MilkMade had a membership model in which people paid up to $30 to have two pints delivered each month. Her first fundraising effort resulted in $47,000 raised on Kickstarter. (Her campaign was cleverly called a "Lickstarter.") MilkMade started with just fifty members in her East Village neighborhood; thanks to her hard work and the new capital, it expanded to the West Village, then all of Manhattan and Brooklyn, and now serves the greater New York City area.

When Diana got her first big order from a national supplier, she needed to make large quantities of ice cream and invest in a better dry-ice shipping solution. She didn't have the capital for this and didn't want to miss the opportunity to sign the big new account, so she raised $300,000 in a seed round from angel investors and used the funds to expand her production capabilities (new kitchen space, new machinery) and bring in two full-time hires. Thanks to the new capital, MilkMade was able to fulfill the order for the big account, dramatically increasing its pint production and number of members.

## Is Your Company Scalable?

*Scalable* is a term that gets thrown around a lot in the business world, so it's worth taking a moment to define it. Being scalable means that your business (or part of your business) has an operations-to-revenue ratio that gives it the potential to bring in revenues that are disproportionately higher than the staff or resources needed to capture that revenue.

A scalable company, simply put, is one where you can sell a lot more widgets (or subscriptions or services) in many more places (typically nationally or internationally) while drawing on the same number of staff or have only a small increase in staff. If it's just you selling and working with clients—as in a consultancy, where you are the consultant and what you are selling is your time—that is not scalable, unless you can train other people to do what you do and provide more services at minimal additional cost in overhead and staff. For a great book that addresses the A to Z of building a scalable business, read Verne Harnish's *Scaling Up*.

In my own case, Little Pim is scalable because once we produced our videos, we were able to sell them all over the world without adding many more staff or having to produce new goods. We went from $500,000 to $1 million in revenues with just three full-time staff and a handful of consultants and interns. Whether we sold in twenty stores or two hundred, I needed relatively few additional full-time employees or infrastructure.

All businesses are different, and not all are scalable to the same degree. Women are statistically more likely to launch businesses in sectors like health care, social assistance, and education instead of the more scalable industries, like tech, where small investments can fuel massive growth. There are still disproportionately small numbers of women studying STEM subjects, such as engineering and computer science, that lead to the more scalable tech companies. But it's not just about the sectors. For example, some businesses that don't seem like tech businesses (for instance, those that sell a product) can still raise money like those in the tech sector if they are using technology to scale faster.

Many of us don't know how to build what is considered a scalable business or how to find the people who can help us determine the part of our business that could be scalable and easiest to fund. Knowing where you are on the spectrum of scalability can help you understand your company's potential. Advisors and coaches can help you uncover the scalable part of your business; go to the exercises at the end of the book for tools to start that conversation. Once you determine what the scalable idea is in your business, you can work backward to calculate the capital you will need to get there.

## Stefanie Syman of Spark No. 9

Stefanie Syman is a partner at Spark No. 9, a consulting firm that helps businesses attain high growth and increase profitability. Prior to that she cofounded the award-winning online magazine *FEED*, one of the first web media properties, and has been on the founding executive team of several other start-ups. She knows what entrepreneurs experience and has been helping women access capital and increase their chances of business success by implementing new strategies.

### Why aren't women as comfortable asking for money as men are?

It's the confidence gap. Men overestimate their confidence, so when they are going to ask for money they really believe they are going to succeed and create this multimillion-, billion-dollar company. Fundraising is all about selling the vision at scale—not what it is today, what it will be at scale. Very few women do that.

### What's the relationship between being good at raising money and being good at running a company?

There is a belief that the best fundraisers are often not the best CEOs, because they are great at selling the vision but often less able to dig in operationally. Often you have a cofounder who's an inspiring storyteller, and another who's the operations genius. Women are a little bit more socialized to be operators, because we are used to multitasking, especially if you are a mom.

When I was recently on a road trip, we were driving along the highway and there were all of these signs trying to get you to come to this fruit stand. For about a mile leading up to this stand it was "Best oranges!" and "Don't try and pass this stand!" But when we finally pulled up to the fruit stand, it was tiny. That seemed to me like a metaphor for what women sometimes do: spend all this energy building something from scratch and doing tons of marketing. But the vision is small and the result is staying small.

I see almost the reverse: people build a huge fruit stand and they don't spend any money trying to figure out the marketing to get people there! Even worse, they make all sorts of assumptions about their customers and never test them.

### Who inspires you?

I love the American Girl story. Pleasant Rowland was in her forties when she started it. She had been a success already in her life, but obviously not at the scale of the American Girl, and she just went out and did it. If your vision is really detailed, it's easier to be tough. She said she had the business in her heart in incredibly fine detail. She founded it in 1986, and in 1998 she sold it to Mattel for $700 million.

# 3. WHERE DO I LEARN THE FUNDRAISING DANCE?

Let's remember what this is really about for our investors: money. They are in it to make a return, and your job is to make them feel like you are the surest bet for getting that return. There is great competition for investment dollars, so you want to be sure you have the right moves before you get out there.

Having worked for five years in the nonprofit fundraising world, I knew *that* dance, how to attract high-net-worth individuals and inspire them to make five- and six-figure donations, but I discovered that the venture capital dance has a whole different set of moves. Some of the steps I learned over time include the following:

- The right way to approach a VC initially is to ask for advice, not to say you're looking for money.
- Never email a VC cold. You must have an introduction. VCs are known to think that if you can't figure out how to get to them, you are probably not worth funding.
- You need a polished pitch deck that tells a great story about your company.
- Pitch with 100 percent confidence.
- Know your numbers and the story they tell. Lines like "Our EBITDA in 2019 is $14 million because 75 percent of our revenues will be in our highest margin channel" need to roll off your tongue.

While learning the dance is a good way to make fundraising feel more approachable, you need to make sure you fully understand the economic dynamics of your business: where the greatest risks are and where you can find economies of scale. A successful financing is one where management and investors work like a team that has a clear and shared understanding of the opportunity and how to go after it. That way, if this or that assumption turns out to be wrong, the team is more likely to remain in synch.

After nine months of pitching in person, by phone, at conferences, and anywhere else that would allow me to, I learned about Golden Seeds. I thought they would be my best partner, since they fund women CEOs and had a lot of other companies in their portfolio selling to our same demographic—great for cross-marketing opportunities. But I didn't know anyone at Golden Seeds. At a playdate for my son I discovered that the mom, who was a friend, had briefly joined Golden Seeds as an investor and still had connections there. She made an email introduction, and just like that I was on their radar. Even better, it turned out they were accepting applications to pitch to their 150 members in less than four weeks.

I prepared like crazy for that meeting. That was when I hired Bill Smartt to be my public-speaking coach, and we spent hours refining my talking points and working on my delivery, cadence, and body language. On the day of the pitch, I looked through the glass window into the amphitheater I'd be pitching in. There were 100 to 150 people, a number of them former Wall Street women who had come up in the hard-numbers world and had run departments, divisions, and companies across numerous industries. I caught part of the previous woman's pitch and thought, *She's so good. Do I have to do that?* She was very powerful, with a booming voice I could hear through the door. I was definitely intimidated. Okay, I was petrified. I knew I had to channel my inner Oprah—I had to think that even if it feels like I am being over the top, it doesn't look that way (as Bill always insisted). Watching the other speaker made me realize, *I have to project the same kind of confidence.*

Once I got in there, I felt a surge of adrenaline and positive energy. I silently reminded myself what a privilege it was to be there, which always calmed my nerves, and tried to be in the moment. My Little Pim logo was up on the big screen in three places—the first slide of my deck. I remembered to look at individual people and not glance at the screen as I pressed the clicker in my right hand. I could hear Bill in my head saying, "Don't scan the room. Deliver a few lines to one person and then a few to another person." One of his lessons was "Let it land" when you make a statement. "Don't be afraid to take a pause." My allotted ten minutes flew by as I walked the audience through our proprietary method and distribution channels and let them know that we were seeking $2 million to scale up and expand our digital offerings. I ended right on time.

I saw a few women smiling broadly at me, which was a big boost, and they applauded in what seemed a genuine way. I felt it had gone well, and I had actually enjoyed walking around the room, making brief connections with members of the audience and sharing my story. Their positive response made me feel much bigger than I had felt walking in. (Three-inch heels also helped.)

Then there was a ten-minute Q&A. I had brought with me my senior VP of sales, Alyson. I deferred some of the questions about our mass retail plans to her, knowing the audience would want to see who was on the team. She sounded knowledgeable as she walked them through our plans for getting into Toys 'R' Us and other mass retailers. I believed we'd done a good job.

Next came the waiting. We waited with feigned coolness in the hall as they voted on our pitch. We were told ahead of time that if they wanted to keep talking to us, we would go into a two-hour session called "Deep Dive," where the ten or so people most interested in our deal would delve into our business. We were invited to stay. And we got through that too. Things were starting to look hopeful.

A few days later we learned that we'd passed to the next step: due diligence. This is the part of the dance where the potential investors review your contracts, as well as your past financials and records, to the tune of more than fifty documents. After much holding of breath and uploading of what felt like endless documents to their online portal, we passed! Golden Seeds gave us a term sheet, the summary of the deal they were offering in exchange for investment. After another five weeks of negotiating, we were close to a deal. In a final twist, they asked to trade lowering my valuation (the company's stated worth) by half a million dollars in exchange for closing quickly, in August. That would give them a bigger stake in the company. I took it.

Why August? Because I really needed the money before September in order to shore up our marketing budget for end-of-year sales. We earned some 40 percent of our annual revenues during the holiday season, and marketing dollars spent in Q2 and Q3 could make or break our year in Q4. I accepted, and they put in the first $1 million. With that in place, I raised another $600,000 from existing investors. Another $500,000 came from a matching grant from the New York State Innovate Fund. When all was said and done, I had spent over a year fundraising and raised $2.1 million. I had sold 20 percent of my company in exchange for this new capital.

The funds allowed me to hire three new staffers, triple my marketing budget, and launch new digital products. I felt totally reenergized about Little Pim. I floated into work after the close and felt I was finally running the company the way I had always dreamed of running it. I was able to bring on a top-tier VP of sales and had the product development budget to create new digital products that would allow us to transition the business into a digital content company.

However, the money was not a magic wand that solved all my problems; in fact I had a whole new set of problems: producing complex, financials-heavy quarterly reports for shareholders and hitting aggressive sales targets. But it did get me into the big leagues, and that felt great. I rested on my laurels for about two weeks, took my staff and advisors to dinner at a trendy restaurant, and then went right back to networking and team building.

## Money Real Talk

Here is my checklist for successful fundraising:

- Adopt the right mindset.
- Get the skills.
- Find your flying buttresses.
- Get ready to kiss a lot of frogs.

To raise any kind of capital, you will need to learn to speak convincingly about "the business of your business." We sometimes are so enamored with our product that we spend a disproportionate amount of time explaining it, and in the process short-change the financials and business model. But you need to speak business. As Brian S. Cohen, chairman of New York Angels, says, "I don't want to know about your product. I want to know about your business."

You need to know your monthly burn rate (how much cash you are going through each month after you deduct monthly revenues), your cost of acquiring a customer, and in which sales channels you have the highest margins. Some of these key financials need to get baked into one or two financials slides in your pitch deck. Then you should be ready to spend a few minutes giving additional color when you are pitching, by providing additional financial stats in person. If you aren't sure which stats will impress your potential funder, watch a few entrepreneurs pitch on *Shark Tank*. And if, after all that, you don't know the answer to a question you are asked about your financials, have a stock phrase ready. I used "That is a great question. I will look into it and get back to you."

These are the four Ps you need to be able to articulate to investors:

- Passion: You have to be an evangelist for your company.
- Product: You have to make it unique and timely and price it correctly.
- People: You have to have the best people you can afford and find a way to bring on the best people you can't afford.
- Petrol: You have to ask for the cash you need to go farther faster.

If your pitch deck and in-person presentation convey powerfully what your company is today—referencing all the points above—and what it will become in five or ten years, you will dramatically increase your chance of getting funded. Another key to success is your ability to describe the money-making machine in your business, the parts of your business that generate predictable, recurring revenues via sales and marketing tactics you have tested. With this information, the investor who puts $1,000 into this machine can be relatively certain that it will generate ten to twenty times that amount when the company sells, and the $1,000 will become $10,000 or $20,000. The key part of that sentence is "relatively certain." Investing in start-ups is risky, and many investors never see a return, no matter how promising the business looked at first blush. It's your job to help them see the exciting future you see. You will be one of hundreds of entrepreneurs pitching them, and they will be looking for excuses to dismiss you. Don't give them any.

And yet, even if your pitch is brilliant, you will still be rejected, probably a whole lot of times. A good rule of thumb in fundraising is to expect fifty nos for every yes. Keeping that in mind, I tried to see each no as getting me one step closer to a yes. Kissing frogs is a good metaphor, as is apartment hunting. You can't avoid looking at ten to fifteen apartments in order to find the one you really love. Nor should you skip getting the ten (or fifty) nos that will lead to a yes. I recently was chatting with a woman entrepreneur who said she had pitched four times and gotten four nos and was demoralized and ready to give up. Once she learned that hearing repeated nos was normal, though, she felt ready to get back out there and kiss a few more frogs.

## Prepare, Prepare, Prepare

I was pretty nervous about everything I needed to learn to be VC-ready, so I decided to approach it like learning a new language. After all, that is what we teach at Little Pim, and it is something I have done many times before. In my twenties I spent two months living in Berlin, studying German at a school in the morning and going out for hours of beer-drinking in the evening, where I would recombine the thirty words I had learned that day in as many ways as possible. It didn't faze me a bit. In fact learning German felt like an adventure! I tried to channel that same spirit when I went after venture capital.

I read *Venture Deals: Be Smarter Than Your Lawyer and Venture Capitalist* by Brad Feld and Jason Mendelson and *The Fundraising Rules* by Mark Peter Davis, which gives you actual fully formed responses you can use when answering tough questions from VCs. I watched how-to-pitch videos on YouTube, studied episodes of *Shark Tank*, talked to fellow CEOs about their experiences raising money, asked my business-whiz cousin Justin for tips, went to practice meetings with low-priority VCs in order to have a chance to make mistakes, and basically became "conversational" in the language of venture capital. I learned the difference between preferred and common stock, and about valuations, liquidation preferences, raising in tranches, and more (see glossary). The process was much more doable than I had imagined once I got focused and cleared the space in my mind and in my professional life. (I am so grateful to my team, who carried the lion's share of operations during that time and cheered me on.) In preparing to raise venture capital you should do what works for you—read books, take an online or in-person class, talk to other CEOs. Just don't try to wing it.

Once you know the language, you need to find your own personal style. Do you need to pitch with bravado, or can you get the check with a softer approach? Adam Quinton, an active early-stage investor, says, "When it comes to leadership behaviors, there is plenty of evidence that women suffer the double-bind—a sort of damned-if-you-do, damned-if-you-don't scenario." Too often people see women as great team players but not as leaders. And when women start acting "more like men," they typically come across as "bossy" or "unlikeable." The only answer I have to this conundrum is don't try to fake anything and don't worry so much about being liked. Adam says, "If you're authentic and know your stuff, that will come through." Spend your effort becoming confident and knowledgeable, not aping male swagger. If you need a power boost, you can check out Amy Cuddy's TED Talk, where she teaches "power poses" you can do right before a big presentation that make you feel more confident and ready to own the room.[14]

Will male VCs say inappropriate things? Yes, that could happen. Will you be the only woman pitching at all-male gatherings? Yes, that could happen. My best advice is to focus on making real connections with the people who can help you get funded and don't get hung up on the rest. I always thought of myself as an entrepreneur first, a woman second. Develop good radar for the guys who are bad apples and avoid them, but don't make the mistake of thinking all VCs are hiding worms. And try not to indulge in too much commiserating with other women about the bad apples, tempting as it might be. There are better uses of your time and energy (like learning to speak venture capital).

One advantage of being a woman entrepreneur is that we are still largely the exception when we are meeting VCs, so we often get top billing. Many VCs have seen the studies highlighting the ways that companies with women on the board or at the helm actually perform better than companies with all-male leadership teams, which get a lot of play in *Forbes* and the *Wall Street Journal*. But there still aren't enough women pitching. David

Sze, a partner at the Silicon Valley firm Greylock (backers of Facebook, LinkedIn, and Pandora), says about 10 percent of the entrepreneurs he sees each year are women. When I expressed surprise at how low that number was, he pointed out that his firm, which actively tries to fund with an eye to diversity, sees the most women of all the firms in Silicon Valley!

## My Pitches

Even unsuccessful pitches can pay dividends. I was invited to a venture capital roundtable at *Forbes* with four or five VCs and five other entrepreneurs. We each had one minute to present our product and do our ask. I spent hours preparing that one minute, including a two-hour session with my public-speaking coach. All the VCs were men, but a couple of them had young children, and they seemed to "get" Little Pim. They even voted it the best pitch of the roundtable. But it didn't lead to any funding. I met several times with one of the investors who attended, but in the end he was not able to convince the general partners at his firm to come along. That happened to me more than once. If you're not dealing with someone who's a decision maker you can waste a lot of time. The only silver lining is that thanks to that roundtable, I met the editor of the *Forbes* entrepreneur channel. He asked me to become a *Forbes* blogger, which was a strong asset in my personal profile for attracting investors. And I'm still blogging for *Forbes* today.

Another time, I pitched a private banker with venture capital contacts who someone on my board set me up with. He was my age and raising French-speaking kids, so we had a lot in common. He liked what he knew about Little Pim, but when he brought me in to pitch, his boss, an Israeli gentleman in his sixties, did not see the appeal. He kept calling our program CDs instead of DVDs and said he really couldn't understand why parents would pay for language learning. He was pretty blunt in his opinion that Little Pim wouldn't work. It was clear in the first ten minutes that he had not bought into language teaching for young kids as a business, and nothing we could say would sway him. I'd prepared for days. I'd brought my team members. We were all fired up. It was totally deflating. But that is part of the dance too.

I found the best way to get through all these pitches was to remind myself of three things on the way in the door:

1. *I have done something remarkable.* The investors may have the capital I need to build my business, but I have created a company from scratch. That is something they may never have done, and if they have done it, then they know how hard it is and we should be able to have mutual respect.

2. *I am their peer.* When you are fundraising, it is crucial to not feel you are starting with a power imbalance. This can be tough if there is a big age spread or if you get the sense you're meeting with five guys who are millionaires and you're not sure if you can pay yourself next month. But I always try to remember that without me, they don't have a business. They need me as much as I need them.

3. *Show them the gold.* In all my fundraising, nonprofit and for profit, I always believed the essence of what I was doing was showing the potential donor or investor the "gold"—the thing about the business that makes it special. You know what the gold is because you see it every day, and it's why you are taking all these risks to create something extraordinary. Your job is to show it to them with language, visuals, financials, and emotions that speak to them.

On the way *out* the door, if I felt I had shown them the gold, knew my numbers, and made a genuine connection with the people in the room, then my job was done. They might choose to invest or not invest for a million reasons. My grandmother Edna used to say about dating, "Every pot finds its lid." Fundraising is no different.

## Leave Them with a Big Idea

If you are going to take away only one thing from this chapter, remember the importance of getting help with your pitching skills. I am convinced the coaching I was fortunate to get from my professional public-speaking coach, Bill Smartt, was key to my successes. Investors are really investing in *you*. The pitch is the make-it-or-break-it moment when they decide if they trust you and believe in your vision. Bill coached me to tell the story of my company in a more compelling way. I learned to start with what inspired me to create Little Pim, to move the parts about the big opportunity to earlier in the pitch, and to leave audiences with a big, exciting idea. Before I met Bill I was ending with something like "I hope you will join us in helping kids learn a second language," but after we worked together, I would wrap up with "We are transforming how children are learning languages all over the world."

Bill also taught me something very basic but extremely valuable: how to say my name in a more deliberate way. Until I began working with him, I always thought I knew how to say my name! Most of us rush through our introductions and the opening of our pitches, due to understandable nerves, but Bill helped me to realize that saying my name loudly and clearly and pausing after I said it helped me establish my power and presence in a way that set me up to "own the room." He also helped me slow down my rapid-fire pace and cut out parts of my story that didn't help the narrative arc about my company and where it was going. An actor by training and a big-hearted southerner by birth, Bill was encouraging and always made me feel I could do this. If I needed to, I could even call him from my hotel room before a big pitch and rehearse my talk on FaceTime.

If you don't have a coach or can't afford one yet, you can start by pitching to friends and colleagues. Then, when you feel ready to get out there, pitch to investors who would never fund you just to learn the kinds of questions they ask. I remember one of my first pitches, telling my Little Pim story on the phone to a VC who had nothing to do with my sector. His firm funded only biotech, but he had kids who were learning languages in school and was doing a favor to a high school buddy of mine by taking the call. Plus, most VCs are naturally very curious. If you approach them in the right way (asking for just a few minutes of their time, getting referred by someone who knows them), they will usually take a call or a short meeting just to hear your idea. The biotech VC asked me tough questions that helped me hone my case for the next time around. And he wound up making an introduction to a friend who did fund companies like mine.

Some funders also hold open office hours. These are a good way to get a foot in the door and a chance to de-bug your pitch. They will often tell you where your pitch is weak and what other information you need to gather before formally presenting. When my friend Kara, who runs a Saas (software as a service) company, went to open office hours at a venture capital firm in New York, she learned that her pitch sounded like a lot of her competitors' pitches. She realized that she needed to find a way of describing her business that made it stand out.

## Getting to Yes

The good news for women is that increasing numbers of VCs would rather see a woman pitch than yet another twenty-three-year-old Stanford guy in a hoodie. Still, the numbers show that those same VCs are still more likely to *invest* in the guy in the hoodie, so be aware that you still need to be twice as good in order to get the VCs over their conscious and unconscious biases about what an entrepreneur looks and sounds like. Women who have successfully raised venture capital usually agree that wearing simple and classy attire and jewelry that is not too distracting is the best way to make sure the audience is focused on your business, not your baubles, or worse, your boobs. If you do meet with discrimination, try to move on quickly and know that success is the sweetest revenge. The venture capital world is tiny, and it's best not to spit in that soup while you are still sipping it.

Many women with consumer-focused companies found the VCs they were pitching to did not understand their target customers or the market they were trying to reach. Studies show that venture capital firms with women partners are more than three times as likely to invest in companies that have women CEOs. But very few venture capital firms have women partners, and the numbers of women at the big venture capital firms have been declining, not increasing, over the last decade.[15] The founders of BaubleBar, which sells costume jewelry online, found a creative solution to pitching to rooms of men in Silicon Valley. Amy Jain and Daniella Yacobovsky knew that most VCs would not have much, if any, experience with online shopping for jewelry, so they sent a box of products ahead of time to the (mostly female) receptionists of the VCs they were pitching to. Then they called the women and spoke with them at length about the products. When Amy and Daniella showed up, the receptionists were often wearing the jewelry, and in a few cases the VCs asked them to come in the room and share what they liked about their necklace or bracelet. Bauble-Bar wound up raising $10 million from a variety of investors, including J. Christopher Burch, cofounder of the Tory Burch empire. That was a great example of showing them the gold—quite literally, in this case!

Two women entrepreneurs who created a shopping tool that allows consumers to track when products go on sale did online research about the partners they were pitching to. Then, early in their presentation, they showed a slide that featured one of the partners they were pitching to wearing clothes he already owned available at a discount through their site. He was surprised, and intrigued, that the site had this functionality and seeing his clothing in the pitch made it personal. This kind of creative approach made them really stand out, even with the Rock Dudes.

## 4. HOW MUCH EQUITY AND CONTROL WILL I HAVE TO GIVE UP?

Every day I meet women with great ideas—and modest ambitions. I met Iris at a VC-sponsored party at a Mexican restaurant in downtown Manhattan. Iris is a second-generation Indian American in her late twenties, had attended a top university, and is well spoken and polished. She soon had me totally entranced on the subject of houseplants. She was passionate about the idea of merging houseplant purchasing with an online community and making buying plants for your dorm room, apartment, or house as personalized and fun as Etsy has made buying accessories.

The more she spoke, the more I could picture it. I began thinking she had identified an overlooked market. She was doing a Kickstarter campaign and had pulled in a programmer friend to help her build the Beta site at minimal cost.

"How much are you raising to get this off the ground?" I asked.

"We are trying to raise $13,000," she said.

Really? How far can you get on $13,000? That barely pays for your fees for hosting the site and a few email blasts. In the course of the evening I introduced her to a few different VCs in the room and encouraged her to follow up with them to help her think through her plans and get fresh perspectives on how much capital she would need to get there in a real way.

Iris is at least out there thinking about money and networking in places where she can meet her future investors. But, like Iris, women often shoot so low because they worry about giving up control. I think this is a red herring. Most women who are running large, high-revenue-generating businesses have *more* control over how their companies can grow, not *less*. Of course we have all heard horror stories of investors coming in and over-riding the founder—or, in extreme cases, pushing her out—but the way I see it, my interests are aligned with my shareholders' in that we all want the company to become as successful as possible. The day I think someone can drive Little Pim better than I can, I will gladly move to a different role and help him or her take the company to new heights.

Every deal is different, but you can expect to give up 20 to 30 percent control after you raise your first round of venture capital. Your best source to assess how much of your company you may have to give up in exchange for capital is other CEOs who are willing to share this typically confidential information. Following blogs in publications like *Inc.* and *Forbes* will give you some case studies. Also make sure to vet your angels and VCs with your CEO friends. Don't just let them vet you. Speak with other entrepreneurs who were funded by your potential investor in order to find out the good and bad. It's not overreaching to say your relationship with your VCs will be like a marriage, so think hard about whether they will be the type to blame you for anything that goes less than perfectly or will be willing to dive in and help you do the work.

## Fred Wilson of Union Square Ventures

At the top of the venture-capital food chain, Union Square Ventures manages $1 billion across six funds. Fred Wilson focuses on web service companies and shared his thoughts about how women can pitch successfully. He's also learned from his wife, Joanne Wilson, who is an active angel investor and has supported many women-run companies.

**When you think of successful women entrepreneurs, what comes to mind?**

In many instances, women have impressive domain expertise. We funded Elizabeth Iorns, who is the founder of Science Exchange, an eBay-style marketplace for scientific research. People post a request on the science exchange website, and then research laboratories that have the capabilities to do those experiments respond and say, "Hey, we can do that; it will cost $20,000 and it will take us three weeks." Elizabeth was a scientific researcher in the world of academic biology, and she understood the problem and saw the opportunity and went after it. I think a lot of the women who we work with are not entrepreneurs because they woke up one day and said, "I want to start a company," and then started looking around and saying, "What company am I going to start?" They were in an industry doing something and were like "Wow, there is nobody doing this and this needs to happen."

**When is the right time to raise venture capital?**

After you have raised money from angels and seed funds. It's like a ladder: you have got to step on the first rung to get to the second rung and to get to the third rung. Venture capital is the third or forth rung; it's not the first. You can skip ninth grade and go right from eighth grade to tenth grade, but I think you can mess up kids if you do that. Also, you don't want to go out and raise venture capital until you have enough data to convince your existing angel investors and potential venture capital investors that you are going to be able to build something that will ultimately be able to produce hundreds of millions of dollars in revenue. VCs are in the business of investing between $3 million and $20 million to get out between $30 and $200 million. You have to be convinced that the market is big enough to support a business that big.

**It is safe to tell people seeking venture capital to plan on giving up 20 to 30 percent of their company?**

I like to tell entrepreneurs to think about raising money every twelve to eighteen months. Raise enough money every time to fund the company for ideally eighteen to twenty-four months, and never dilute more than 20 percent, but be prepared to always dilute at least 20 percent. In your seed round, you are going to give up between 10 and 20 percent, and hopefully you are going to buy at least a year of runway. In your angel round you are going to give up another 10 to 20 percent, and you are going to hopefully buy eighteen months of runway. In your venture round, you are going to give up 10 to 20 percent and you hopefully are going to buy eighteen to twenty-four months of runway again.

**Once they get venture capital, what can women do to make sure that they stay on that track?**
Perform. Deliver on what you said you were going to deliver on. But I will say something else. There are three kinds of investors. There are bad people who will do harm to your company. There are weak, ineffective people who will do nothing. And there are strong, effective people who will help you immensely.

## Always Growing, Always Fundraising

To get Little Pim into the multimillions-in-revenues realm, I raised three distinct kinds of capital over a five-year period: friends and family, angel, and venture capital. There were only brief periods of time during which I *wasn't* fundraising. And this, in retrospect, made all the difference between staying small and going big. I came to realize that fundraising is not an occasional inconvenience like a head cold. It is a continual and vital part of my job as CEO.

People often asked if I was anxious about giving up equity in the company, but I always said, "Zero percent of zero is zero." In other words, if I didn't take investment, the company would stay small and grow more slowly. I also truly believed I would never get to the big revenue numbers I wanted without investment. I chose to bet on our future success and align with my investors in taking that risk.

There is a saying among fundraisers: "The best time to raise money is when you don't need it." That's because fundraising is about relationships, and these take time to build. If you suddenly realize on January 15 that you'll be out of cash by March 15, or you can't fulfill an order without placing a big inventory order, you may not have enough time to find, cultivate, and close a new investor. Whereas if you've been friends with an army of great potential investors for a decade, they are just a phone call away and you could have the cash in the bank that very week.

Part of the reason many women do not have access to capital for their companies is they don't have a pool of potential investors to draw from, so when it comes time to bring in another $50,000, $100,000, or $1 million, they have to start from nothing, and it's just too big a lift. You need to have a strong network to draw from when capital needs arise.

If your company is in the tech space or has a tech component, it might qualify for one of the thousands of accelerators and incubator programs throughout the country, such as TechStars and Y Combinator.[16] These programs are mainly for pure tech companies and are highly selective. They take less than 1 percent of the applicants, but if you are admitted, you get some actual cash ($40,000 to $100,000), a community of other entrepreneurs, training in fundraising, advisors and mentors, and introductions to investors and industry leaders. They take a percentage of your company's equity (5 to 9 percent) in exchange for the services and mentorship they provide.

Regardless of the type of investor you are approaching—angel, venture capital, family fund, or your cousin Greta—you need to inspire them with your passion, dedication, and big vision for your company. Brian Cohen, chairman of the much-sought-after group New York Angels, sums it up: "Before I write you a check, I want to feel something."

## Ed Zimmerman, Venture Capital Lawyer

One of the best venture capital lawyers in the United States, Ed Zimmerman represents start-ups at every stage of a company's life and has been an angel investor in more than thirty companies. As a leader in the world of venture capital, he has made the scarcity of female entrepreneurs a central issue, and he's found ways to make a difference. As a professor of venture capital in the MBA program at Columbia Business School, he trains the men in his classes to not talk over the women and the women to speak up. As a mentor, he has started clubs for junior venture capital women and brought senior women in to have lunch with them. He's one of the good guys.

### How do you see gender issues manifest?

I had this interesting experience when I first invested in Birchbox and Bauble-Bar—and both of those companies are doing extremely well—where a lot of guy investors would be introduced to the company and say, "Can you talk to my wife?" We just represented Birchbox raising $60 million, and now men walk up to the founders at parties and say, "Hey! I asked you to talk to my wife. You never followed up. I just should have invested. I'm sorry I missed it." One of the founders said, "Yeah, we didn't follow up because we were looking for investors who got it, rather than investors who wanted us to talk to their wives."

### What do you think women entrepreneurs should do differently to secure venture capital?

Let's take a situation where you go around the table and talk about yourselves. I was in one event where we all went around the table and did the "Here is the ninety-second version of who I am," and one of the most celebrated and impressive people at the table was the founder and CEO of a company that I had invested in. When she said who she was and what she did, it was the most diminished, meek, humble version of who she was. I told her later, "You are one of the most impressive people I know. Why is it not okay to say that you have won this award and that award and you have achieved this and that? Why isn't that okay?" She said she wasn't comfortable. She was like "I know I've done it. I don't need to tell the rest of the world." My answer was "Your Wikipedia page tells the rest of the world. It's not a secret."

### Are men different in that respect?

When the boys talk they are incredibly proud of their achievements. The first day of each year that I teach at Columbia, I ask a hypothetical question within the first thirty minutes of class, and in order for me to achieve the result I am seeking, I must get someone to provide a wrong answer. And I always do, because I always call on the guy who raises his hand first. Women are sitting pondering, because they are afraid to say that the question has information missing. But the men are not fraught with self-doubt the way the women are. There are gender differences that pop up. Women sometimes don't show the same bravado I see in guys. I even see it with my two kids. They both started on swim teams. In my son's first heat, he was horrible, poor kid. He came out of the water and people were laughing. I said to my son, "When you came out of the water, were you breathing like this?" [*Heavy breathing.*] He said, "No." And I said, "Well, that is not really racing, is it? Because when you race you try to get really, really fast." He is like "Yeah, but I did a great job." My daughter came in second out of 107 people in another race, which is awesome, and she walks out of the water and says, "Oh my God! I am terrible." I see that in venture capital all day long.

# 6

# SLIP INTO SOMETHING MORE COMFORTABLE:

## INTENTIONAL NETWORKING

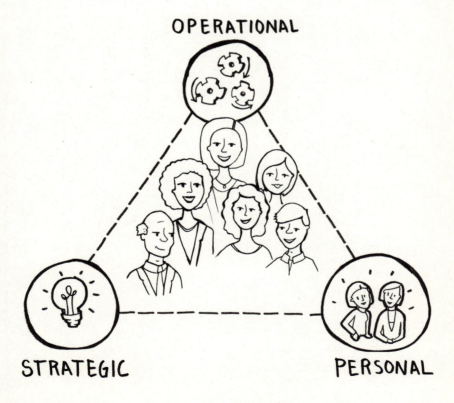

Carla Harris, vice chair and managing director at Morgan Stanley and author of the inspirational business books *Expect to Win* and *Strategize to Win*, says that in your twenties and thirties, what makes you stand out in the business world is your competence, but in your forties and fifties, it's your network. This is an area where I've noticed that women tend to come up short. Many of us consider ourselves very *social*, in both the traditional and the online meaning of the word, but we aren't always very *strategic* about how we spend our time and with whom. We might even think putting "strategic" in the same sentence as "social" sounds sort of sleazy.

According to the *Harvard Business Review*, to succeed as a leader, you need to build three types of networks:

1. Operational: people who can accomplish routine tasks.
2. Personal: kindred spirits who can help you move forward.
3. Strategic: people who will challenge you to reach objectives.

Most of us are pretty good on the operational and personal networks but may fall short when it comes to the strategic.[1] In order to grow personally and professionally, we need to embrace what I call "intentional networking," which embraces a bit of all three types of networking. As the acclaimed speaker Josh Klein points out in his TED Talk, "Invest in Your Network and They Will Invest in You," some of us resist the idea of networking because it sounds like, "We are going to interact so that we can get maximum economic value out of each other!" That sounds so icky that we want to take a shower. But in a world where information is free and instantly available and labor is cheap and often offshore, our networks have become one of our most valuable assets in the professional marketplace. Who you know and who trusts you will determine what projects you can get done, what circles of power you have access to, and ultimately what level of success you can achieve.

# KEEP YOUR SCHEDULE, DON'T LET IT KEEP YOU

How are you going to build your own strategic network and become a more *intentional* networker? According to research, most women start their business when they are in their thirties, so they may also have a partner or spouse, and many have young children or aging parents. This means there are a lot of demands on their time, piled onto the pressures of building a business. I get it. I had a toddler at home when I started Little Pim, and I was pregnant with my second child when we were signing our first deal with a national retailer and scaling up. Now that my kids are six and nine, it's a little bit easier to find some wiggle room, but I still want to be very present in their lives, all while running a high-growth business. Making time for intentional networking isn't easy. Everyone's schedule will present different challenges. But if you don't keep an intentional schedule, your haphazard schedule will keep you!

Once I decided to take Little Pim to the next level, I took a hard look at how I was spending my time outside of work and with whom I was having breakfast, coffee, and lunch on a regular basis. I decided to get more purposeful about how I spent those hours. I love systems and take any chance I can get to geek out with a spreadsheet, so I decided to create an "outreach chart" in Excel, where I kept track of the people I met who could help me propel my business forward in a variety of areas. I kept the spreadsheet right on my desktop, looked at it every day, and made sure my head of operations, Jeremy, had access to it. Jeremy and I had daily check-ins about setting up meetings, and I made sure he knew which were coffees, which were lunches, and which were calls I could take after my kids had gone to bed.

My outreach chart included fellow CEOs, advisors, people I meet at conferences or who contacted me through social media, board members, and mentors. I made it a point to have lunch or breakfast with one or two of them each week (the chart helped me sort to highest priority via a 1 to 3 rating system), and I tracked follow-up items in the spreadsheet. Each event I attended had its own tab, with the people I met and how and when I needed to follow up with them. If your own inner spreadsheet geek is hibernating, feel free to use my outreach chart template, which you can find at juliapimsleur.com along with other options for keeping your contacts organized.

Whatever system you use, use one. It's important to find a way to keep track of your network, whether via free Google tools or an off-the-shelf customer relationship management system like Salesforce or a business-card scanning app that catalogues business cards digitally. If you don't have a plan, you will likely get quickly overwhelmed trying to find business cards in your purse and remember who people are, when they said they would be back in town, and even why you wanted to meet them in the first place. If you can still remember by name all the people you are meeting, you probably need to kick up your networking a notch.

The other way to ensure you are not the smartest person in the room is to fill that room you spend the most time in—your office—with people who are experts in their fields. I have always had a "hire up" policy. When interviewing for senior staff, I make sure to hire people who know more than I do. Sometimes this means hiring someone only part time because I can't afford his or her full-time rate. (Our first national distribution deal came from an introduction made by my first marketing hire, a talented veteran of the publishing industry I could afford only three days a week.) My current Senior VP of sales, Alyson, has fifteen years of experience in retail, digital, and children's products under her belt and has taught me so much about selling online and working with big retail chains. She leads our sales team far better than I could. Similarly our VP of finance is a whiz with shareholder reports and investor decks and figuring out gross margins. Thanks to working closely with her, I can figure them out too, and love tracking which products are yielding better returns.

## JOIN AN OLD BOYS' CLUB AND CHANGE IT

I have already sung the praises of EO, my entrepreneurs' group, which is 10,000 strong, with 240 in New York City. At EO events, I am not the smartest person in the room, and I like it that way. I've learned best practices from entrepreneurs who are ahead of where I am—like how to structure bonuses for sales people, which cloud storage to use for our company, and how to run more efficient board meetings.

I made friends with people in EO I likely would not have met through my own social circles—most of them men in their forties and fifties running successful businesses. The fact that we are all founding CEOs is a powerful bond that generally trumps gender, race, and class. However, only about 12 percent of EO members are women, so I am often one of just a handful of female members at board meetings and learning events. That was the only part of EO that I didn't love—I really missed connecting with other women CEOs who were facing the same challenges I was. To bring in more women and make sure we could all find one another in this sea of guys, I started a women's group within EO called EO Ellas (*ellas* is the plural for *she* in Spanish). These women have become some of my greatest allies and friends in business-building and in life. We meet for drinks, bring in authors to speak to us, share war stories, and have dinner in one another's homes. The existence of EO Ellas has attracted impressive new female members to EO too, and our friendships make the sometimes awkward, sometimes demoralizing moments we still experience as CEOs and within EO easier to laugh off.

The EO Ellas concept is now spreading to other EO chapters. At the 2015 Global Leadership Conference, we had the first all-women leaders from around the world luncheon and challenged EO to get the number of women in the organization to 20 percent by 2020. Other EO Ellas chapters have been springing up around the country and around the world. I had the privilege of attending the inaugural EO Ellas in London. It was a thrill to find our UK counterparts having the same conversations we are having here in New York about how to raise capital, be true to our families, and run successful businesses—and do it all in a way that feels authentic as women.

## Carla Harris of Morgan Stanley

Carla Harris is the vice chair and managing director at Morgan Stanley. President Obama appointed her chair of the National Women's Business Council, an advisory panel that counsels the president and Congress about issues important to women entrepreneurs. NWBC is the government's only independent voice for women entrepreneurs; its members are women business owners and leaders of women's business organizations across the country.

### How important is networking?

In your twenties and thirties, what matters most is performance currency, which is about how you do your job—are you good at it? Having a reputation of always delivering is important. Performance currency gets you recognized, gets you paid and promoted, and may attract a sponsor for you because you are so known out there as being really good at what you do. But as you get more senior in your career, it is really all about the relationships, because your ability to move up is a function of somebody's judgment: *Can Julia handle this? Is she ready for this challenge? Will she motivate the team?* Your career at that stage is linked to your ability to influence a decision-maker based on your relationships.

### How do you nurture those kinds of relationships?

You don't have to go out and meet people all the time. You just have to continue to find ways to stay in front of people. The Internet is a beautiful thing. Let's say you find fourteen relationships that you are interested in—one of the things that I tell my mentees is, once a quarter, drop each of them a line. Say "Hey, Julia, I can't believe the fall is here. Can you believe how quickly it is coming! Had a great summer. Hope you had a great summer too. I would love to connect before the holidays descend upon us." Then "Happy holidays! Hope you and your family have a great time." Now it is the first quarter: "We are getting going in 2015. I would love to come and talk to you about what I am doing, maybe sometime later in the spring." Now you are into the second quarter. I have had three touches in less than six months, all by Internet. So we didn't talk. We didn't meet. But you probably read your email, and you might have even emailed me back. We had a point of touch. So when I get ready to sit down with you in April and now talk to you about my business plan, you are not reaching back to when we met sometime in August or September.

### What advice do you have for women about going out and meeting people?

I always draw up a plan and say, "What does success look like if I go into this meeting, or if I go into this cocktail party?" Success is "I got to connect with these ten people," or success is "I am going to get ten business cards." If it is a huge conference and I don't know anybody, then I am not being discriminating about which cards. I just tell myself I want to get the tenth card because these are all asset allocators, for example.

Or if they are specific people, then I say, "I am going to make sure I touch these ten people." I have an agenda that I am going to articulate. So if I am meeting Julia and I want to be able to have a sit-down with her, then I say, "I want to meet Julia. Success is to tell her that I am going to follow up the next day and get her to agree that I can get on her calendar."

### How do we learn the right dance steps for things like venture capital pitch meetings?

Every job has a kind of uniform, and raising capital is no different. You've got to make sure that if you are walking into an industry where there is a norm around—how do you speak, how do you dress, how do you present—you want to make sure that you demonstrate an understanding of that. You may choose to do it a little bit differently, so in a room full of blue suits you may choose to wear red that day, but you better bring it, right? What you want to demonstrate is "I know how you play and understand the rules of your game, but I want you to come with me for a while, walk with me for a second."

I feel like women really have a lot of work to do on getting right up front: "Here is why I am here. Here is what I have to offer."

I think if you are with an audience where you feel like you need to have a credential, then you might want to put that up front, but I am not a big fan of having to wear your résumé on your sleeve. You've got to be careful, because it may seem like you are justifying why you are there. It should be "I don't need to justify why I am here because if I sent my material to you ahead of time and you had a chance to go through it ahead of time, I am going to assume you read it. If I talk to you for five minutes and I figure out you didn't, then I am going to work it in there so we don't feel uncomfortable about that." And then I am a big fan of putting why you are there up front: "Here is my agenda. This is what we have come to do." People appreciate that—especially busy people. One of the things I tell entrepreneurs all the time is that the two most important questions you can answer when you are making a presentation are "Why me?" and "Why now?"

# SPEND 80 PERCENT OF YOUR TIME OUT OF THE OFFICE

Networking is particularly important when you are seeking to expand your company aggressively. Leading CEOs know the importance of attending conferences, networking with other CEOs, meeting with advisors, and seeking out industry leaders. This is where you will get ideas that are crucial to how you innovate and stay ahead of the curve.

It's tempting to hunker down in tough times and pull up a chair next to your top sales person, but if you listen to business coach Verne Harnish, who has worked with thousands of successful companies, he insists that leading CEOs actually spend 80 percent of their time *out of the office*. You need to have a senior team who can handle the day-to-day in order to free you up to meet your next hire, trade ideas with other leading CEOs, meet potential investors, and keep up with changes in your industry. I can trace about 25 percent of the new business we have done in the past three years to introductions made for me by other CEOs and various advisors with gatekeepers in publishing, digital distribution, and large retail chains.

Staying current in your field and coming up with new ideas inspired by these conversations means you might be the first to market with a new product or can pivot your business to better meet the demands of your customers, and you will have a huge advantage over your competitors. Where do you find those new ideas? Rarely on multicolor Post-Its while sitting at your desk.

I know what you are thinking: "I don't have time to reach out to all these people, book appointments, and be out of the office." Especially if you have young kids at home or other personal responsibilities you want to devote yourself to, more time can seem like more than you can manage. I have three words for you: *Get an assistant*. If you can't afford a full-time assistant, share one with members of your senior team or hire a virtual assistant (see chapter 7). It's likely your senior team members are also doing things that could and should be outsourced, so sharing an assistant could free them up to do more strategic work.

Setting up meetings is one of the most time-consuming things we do and one of the most undermining of our full potential. The best way to think of it is this: each time you go back and forth via email or phone with a potential lunch or coffee date, you are *cheating* your company. That is precious time you could have spent keeping up with industry trends or cultivating a relationship with a new advisor, strategic partner, or funder. Just because we women are good at multitasking doesn't mean we should keep doing *everything*. We have to say no to some things in order to make room to do what only we can do, and what really matters. I love the expression "Every great yes is defended by a thousand tiny nos."

I admit that when I first handed off my calendar to my assistant I felt like I was acting high and mighty and wondered if my staff would agree. But then I managed to pull myself out of that unproductive female quicksand thinking and reminded myself I was not being paid to schedule appointments. It turned out my staff was thrilled that I had brought someone on full-time so that I could be networking more and bringing us more new business and opportunities.

When I was in my twenties working for other people, especially for women, I looked at them and wondered, *Does she have a life I would want?* When you hire an assistant or take the time to go to your child's school play, you are sending a message to your staff that you have created a life that works for you. I believe they would prefer to see us thriving than working night and day without any balance. Otherwise what are they aspiring to? I actually left my filmmaking career in part because I looked at the women producers who were ten years ahead of me and realized I didn't want the life I saw most of them leading, with financial insecurity, few intact families, even fewer children, and a lot of travel and stress. I'd rather have my staff see me enjoying my role as CEO, meeting with industry leaders, making time for my family, and generally working smarter rather than harder.

## IF YOU DON'T HAVE AN ADMIN, YOU ARE THE ADMIN!

We frequently have to staff up or develop new products to land a big new account, and setting ourselves up for networking success is no different. Initially I had my assistant Jeremy for three days a week and would save my scheduling for those days. But when I set out to raise venture capital I knew I was going to be doubling my number of meetings and needed his help to keep track of all the new names and companies so that I could be free to focus on the content of the meetings. So I brought Jeremy on full time in anticipation of my success. It was one of the best decisions I've ever made.

Handing over my calendar did three things: (1) it gave me back about 30 percent of my work time to use for more productive things like fundraising; (2) it let me enjoy networking more because I no longer dreaded reaching out to people and engaging in the inevitable back and forth of scheduling; and (3) it sent the message that as the CEO of a growing company, my time was valuable.

Very few Million Dollar Women schedule their own appointments; they are über-focused on the three other things. (Remember VC Fred Wilson's advice: "Hire the best people, set the strategy, and keep cash in the bank.") Highly successful people understand that if you don't delegate administrative assistant tasks, then you are effectively the administrative assistant! The most successful leaders are quick to respond to email within twenty-four to forty-eight hours. This gets more and more challenging as you ramp up your business and have increasingly high volumes of email, which is why you want to start learning now how to hand off to someone else. If you don't think your budget has room for a part-time employee or even a virtual assistant, try an online scheduler app like Calendly, Doodle, or YouCanBook.me as an interim step.

## BE SELFISH *AND* GENEROUS WITH YOUR TIME

Any CEO of a growing company will have to make hundreds of choices about which networking opportunities are worth attending, and mastering this skill will become increasingly important as you expand your business and get invited to more functions.

We are all so busy managing our businesses that even just choosing which events to go to can seem overwhelming. When deciding which to attend and which to say no to, I use a mental decision filter. I ask myself what two benefits I will gain from attending, whether I have a chance of accomplishing anything there I am currently working on, and whether I will have a good time. The management guru Stephen Covey created the "Important vs. Urgent Matrix," which helps you prioritize your time.[2]

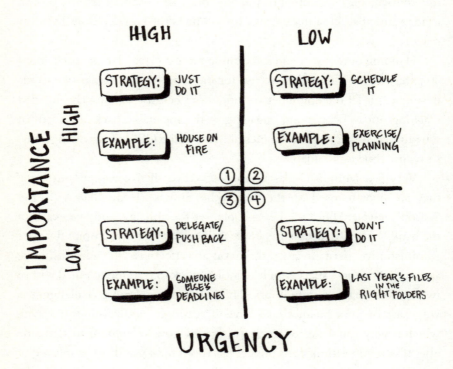

I have my own version that helps me decide which events to go to in any given month. Quadrant 1 is for top-priority events and is reserved for opportunities where I will meet clients or other people who will have a direct impact on helping me grow my business. For example, if I get invited to an event for women business owners, that goes into Quadrant 1 because I will potentially meet new partners for Little Pim (important) and may find someone to fill a new position I am hiring for (urgent), such as director of finance. I consider what my most pressing needs are and whether I will potentially find solutions there. Am I hiring? Raising money? Trying to design a new interactive product? It can feel like a Herculean effort to leave the office before 6:00 to get to an evening event; you will have more luck getting out the door if you know why you are going.

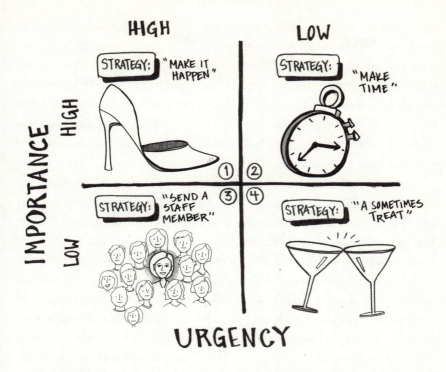

In Quadrant 2 are events that are important for long-term strategy and may require some active research, like attending entrepreneur learning events and going to trade shows or industry-specific conferences. If you are a working mother or just a busy entrepreneur with little time for socializing, you want each of your outings to accomplish more than one thing. There is the fun factor too. Will I see old friends or make new ones? Will I get to see peers and share some laughs? For success in Quadrant 2, you can set yourself up to have ongoing access to these kinds of events. Consider joining a professional organization that has recurring meetings (like EO or BNI or Vistage); you will stay in practice talking about your business, meeting new people, and getting out of the office.

But not all events are a delight, and sometimes you have to just put on your most happening (not painful) high heels and go. I'll never forget going to a Founders' Round Table event a few years ago when I was actively raising my Series B round. Meeting potential investors was a Quadrant 1 top priority. On a bitter cold Monday night in January, I dragged myself after work to this round table in midtown that was usually a place for founding CEOs to mingle. This time there was a guest speaker: an angel investor who was friendly with one of the founders was giving a presentation on what he thought made a good angel investment. During his presentation I learned he had lived in Spain and had three young children, including a newborn. This made him a good potential investor for Little Pim. But as 10 at night came and went, I was getting really tired and was thinking about the long day I had in store and the 5:15 wake-up the next morning with my early-bird son. I just wanted to go home.

After the talk ended, I tried to speak with the investor, but there was a long line and I ultimately gave up. I stopped in the restroom on my way out. There I found myself looking in the mirror and something clicked. The me in the mirror challenged, "You came all this way! You are not going to leave *now* when he is right down the hall!" I took a deep breath and went back to the room. This time the angel investor, let's call him Bob, was standing alone, gathering up his documents, and the line was gone. I introduced myself, and Bob and I had a lovely conversation about the time he spent in Madrid, what he is doing to teach his kids Spanish, my own bilingual background, and of course Little Pim and our current round. He agreed to a follow-up coffee.

Three weeks later (with Jeremy's persistent scheduling help), Bob and I sat down together, and this meeting lasted close to two hours. A month later I had a check for $25,000 and a new passionate investor. A year later I asked Bob if I could use elements of his PowerPoint about what angel investors want in Double Digit Academy, and he said yes. As any good sales person will tell you, to increase your chances of closing on a sale, you need to get the person to start saying yes. Then the chances will be higher that she or he will keep saying it. Start with a coffee. Wind up with a check. And check your Quadrants before you make your evening plans!

## WINNING AT NETWORKING

Then again, meeting people is only half the equation. We all meet people every day, but it doesn't automatically help us get funding or grow as business leaders. I believe that networking that *works* has three components:

1. Genuine and authentic connection.
2. Excellent and timely follow-up.
3. Keeping people engaged over time.

Networking doesn't happen only at industry functions; some of the best connections happen when people are not in business mode. Sometimes a wedding, basketball game, or cookout is where you can make a more authentic connection, when people don't have their professional guard up. You can also use social media to meet people you might not otherwise have access to, by tweeting them at a conference or leveraging a shared contact on LinkedIn. Social media is also a great way to stay connected to people once you have met them. I send out tweets and LinkedIn posts every single day (prepped by my virtual assistant), and it is often the way people I've met keep me top of mind. When they share my tweet or an article I posted, I am back on their radar.

One entrepreneur who raised $3 million for her online shopping company met her biggest angel investor on the private bus that transported them both to a friend's wedding, and another friend found her lead investor on a train ride from New York to Washington, D.C. These encounters were serendipitous, but even in highly formal networking situations like industry conferences that bring out the stuffiness in all of us, you can foster a personal style that is authentic. I have found that one of the best ways of cultivating authenticity is to make sure I am being more inquisitive than informative. It can be tempting to launch right into an elevator pitch, but I try to remember, above all, to be curious about the person in front of me. Not only do I make a more meaningful connection when I do this, but as a byproduct I learn what *they* are passionate about. That way I don't have to guess which part of my business will capture their interest, and can adjust my description accordingly.

Some of the best "elevator pitches" happen when you are not planning on talking business at all. I recently went to an education-technology conference in Arizona and happened to sit on the plane next to Mark, one of the partners from the sponsoring firm. He has his finger on the pulse of the ed tech world as one of the deal makers who sees thousands of companies in this space each year. Mark was working on a PowerPoint that looked like it was related to the conference, and I struck up a conversation based on that. Soon he was asking about my business. The Little Pim story resonated with him since his wife, a TV journalist, spoke several languages and he always wished he had learned. We chatted about language learning, the ed tech industry, how to juggle kids and a career (they were thinking of starting a family), our New York neighborhoods, and good places to get a bite near the conference.

In the course of telling Mark about my business, he came up with several ideas on the spot about how he thought he could be helpful. He had contacts with a major online retailer in China, and also thought his wife, Beth, might be interested in featuring me on her show. One thing to keep in mind about people in the investment world is that they often really enjoy the connecting part of their work. They can invest in only a few companies a year, but they can make a real difference to hundreds of companies by making introductions. Doing these favors also means they have an "in" with your company and you might choose to work with them in a few months or years when you are ready for their services.

I took notes when he made his suggestions and followed up with an email that same day when we landed. When I ran into him at the conference he suggested we sit down and have an actual meeting. He brought one of his partners, who was very interested in our Portuguese since his wife was Brazilian, and we exchanged cards. Though I was not raising capital at that time, it's always good to have two more evangelists, and these guys have broad networks.

The following concrete things happened from that one meeting:

1.   Mark introduced me via email to potential investors at the conference.

2.   Mark introduced me via email a few days after the conference to a Chinese distribution company. This led to a three-way conference call between their head of business development in Beijing, me in New York, and San Francisco, where we explored a distribution deal for Little Pim in China.

3.   He connected me with his wife via email and we had a twenty-minute "get to know you" phone call. End result: she asked to feature me on her show about New York–based businesses.

After each of these interactions I sent Mark a quick close-the-loop email. Here is the email I sent after the conversation with the company in China (names changed):

*Hi Mark,*

*Just a quick shout-out to say thanks again for the intro to Bob at Jeelong. We had a good call last week and they are looking at our English as a Second Language Program right now and considering a partnership. Could be a good win-win for both of us. Beth and I are also set to talk soon. Thanks for being a force of good!*

*Julia*

Mark responded:

*Awesome! Thanks so much for the update Julia—please let me know if I can be of any further help and please do keep me posted. Love what you're doing and can't wait to hear about more successes.*

*Mark*

## MAKE IT EASY FOR PEOPLE TO HELP YOU

I always try to keep communications really short and sweet. People are busy. Effusive thanking is counterproductive. Just a quick "Thanks so much" for the specific favor will do. I also keep a box of high-quality note cards in my desk drawer and try to send handwritten notes when someone has gone out of their way for me or to thank a staff member who has gone above and beyond. In this digital age, I am convinced that print is the new premium. When I want to impress, I resort to good old pen and paper.

If I am asking for a referral or introduction, I always tee it up for them. One of my advisors (now a board member), Steve, told me something so simple but so invaluable in the early days of my business: "Make it easy for people to work with you." I adopted a practice of sending anyone from whom I was asking a favor a draft email and blurb on me and my company. Here is what that process looks like (the example is from an entrepreneur who wanted an introduction to a business owner I know):

*Hi Julia,*

*We took a look at ImageThink and were fascinated—very interesting concept. It seems they offer video animation, so we would like to speak with Heather if you don't mind making the intro. Perhaps you could preface by letting her know we're just two gals in bootstrapping mode at the moment so budget is tight. . . . Below is an email from us to Heather, so if you could forward it along we'd greatly appreciate it.*

    *Thanks again!*

                              *Best,*
                              *Laurie*

*Dear Heather,*

*We learned about ImageThink from Julia Pimsleur who was gracious enough to provide some feedback on growing our start-up, the National Society of Student Professionals (NSOSP). We are an honor society with an online curriculum of skill training for both high school and college students. We would very much like to enhance our website with an animated video and we loved what we saw on ImageThink.*

    *Please let me know when might be a good time for us to chat as we're interested in learning more about your services.*

    *Thanks so much!*

                                *Best,*
                              *Laurie*

I was able to connect Laurie and Heather in seconds because I didn't need to hunt around for a description of Laurie's company or even draft an email—it was all ready to go.

I keep a one-paragraph description of my business, "About Little Pim," in my email drafts (you can use Canned Responses in Gmail—makes it so easy) for quick copying and pasting into these kinds of follow-up emails. Here is a follow-up from a panel I attended (names of people and companies changed):

*Hello Bob,*

*Happy Monday! We met briefly at EO Nerve a couple weeks ago in Philadelphia and you were kind enough to offer to put me in touch with someone at Pendelton.*

*We are expanding our international distribution of Little Pim and considering new ways of exporting our award-winning language teaching method for kids 0-6. I'd love to see if there is a fit with Pendelton, possibly to fill in the early years of your English teaching programs. Ours is the first method designed specifically for kids in the baby, toddler, and preschool years. See the brief description of our company below and a PDF of our retail catalog is attached.*

*If I remember correctly you have young children of your own. I'd be happy to send you a digital download to sample in Spanish, French, Chinese, or any of our 11 languages if you'd like to try it at home!*

*Thanks in advance.*

*Best,*
*Julia*

## About Little Pim

Little Pim is the leading program for young children to learn a second language. The founder and CEO, Julia Pimsleur, is daughter of Dr. Paul Pimsleur, creator of the internationally acclaimed Pimsleur Method. Little Pim's Entertainment Immersion Method® is an award-winning language program for the youngest learners, ages 0–6. The series has won 25 awards and is sold via Direct to Consumer, Retail, and Licensing. Partners include PBS Kidsplay, LeapFrog, VTech, Toys R Us, and Mango Languages. Little Pim is available in 11 languages, is platform agnostic and can be viewed on screens of any size in any country. Future plans include continued international expansion, a new Day Care turnkey teaching program, TV licensing, and expansion at mass retail. See sample content and learn more at LittlePim.com.

He wrote back (same day):

*Julia, thanks for your note. I am copying Henry Ashton, who manages business development for Pendelton.*

> *Best,*
>
> *Bob*

Then I followed up directly with Henry, with a BCC to Bob. This contact at the distribution company might have taken me weeks to find, and I might have gotten blown off even if I had. Instead I got Henry's immediate attention because his colleague had referred me. Nice.

## WHEN IN DOUBT, GET OUT OF THE HOUSE

One entrepreneur told me a great story about how she got her first investment from sitting on an alumni panel she initially wasn't gung-ho about: "I was invited to be on a panel at my alma mater. It was a lot of sixty-five-year-old white men and they wanted diversity, so they were like 'We have this girl and she is younger, so we have two buckets filled!' I was definitely a little more interesting to the students. I talked about my plans for a company, and there happened to be some parents in the audience who started raising their hands and wanting to invest. The moderator turned into an auctioneer, auctioning off my company! Later, I got all these emails, like 'I was serious about that. I want to give you this money.' I called my partner and we said, 'If all these strangers are that excited about it, let's try it.' I quit my job the next day."

Everyone has a different desire and ability to network—and of course not all events lead to walking out with checks in hand!—so you need to find what works for you, and also to push past your comfort levels on occasion. Heather Hiles, the CEO of Pathbrite, doesn't do a lot of networking; instead she spends significant time with four or five hand-picked people who help push her thinking and support her when she needs it. They meet for brunch at least once a month and help one another win new business, make strategic introductions, and stay on track. If that tempts you to ditch networking and invite your three BFFs for Bloody Marys instead, not so fast! Heather became a Million Dollar Woman first, then pared down. In her earlier business-building days she made sure to move in wider circles. That is one of the things she credits for getting her farther faster.

# DELEGATE YOUR
# WAY TO THE TOP

DELEGATION
NINJA

"All failure is a failure of management," said one of my mentors, Pam Wolf, and I could feel the breath *whoosh* out of me as I took this in. Pam and I had been paired up through an EO mentorship program, and she met with me monthly for a year. This statement really stopped me in my tracks, because the implications are so far-reaching. If my customer service person mishandles a call, it's because either I didn't hire well or I didn't train well. If I didn't lower my production costs, it's because I didn't motivate my VP of finance and operations to make that happen. I am the one setting everyone up for success or failure, and I need to own it 100 percent.

If you met Pam, who is a petite, intense, and beautiful woman, you would immediately perceive that she lives by this rule. She is the founder and CEO of New York Kids Club, a highly successful chain of enrichment centers for young children. Being a great manager is part of what makes her excellent at what she does.

As entrepreneurs, we often get used to doing everything ourselves instead of learning to manage and delegate. I know. I had to be the sales person, bookkeeper, and intern rolled into one just to get my businesses off the ground. But to get to the million-dollar revenue mark and beyond, it's much less about multitasking and much more about leading a team. Which means developing a host of leadership and management skills—chief among them, learning to delegate.

As a recovering perfectionist, I know how hard it is to hand over control. I often have to remind myself of the maxim that I hear is pasted on the wall at the Facebook offices: "Done is better than perfect." Delegating is often our Achilles' heel as CEOs. My friend Carrie Kerpen is CEO of Likeable Media, a successful social media agency with thirty full-time employees that has been on the Crain's "Best Places to Work" list six years in a row. Carrie says learning to delegate was one of the hardest and most important things she needed to master: "One of the big things that I needed to do as a leader was eliminate the idea that I am the only person with the 'magic dust' that makes my company run. I used to insist on being in every new business meeting, as well as every client's annual planning—because I and only I could possibly come up with the brilliant idea that would make them millions! I found that this was not only unsustainable, but it diminished the credibility of the great team I had built, *and* it made my company unscalable."

Lululemon's CEO Christine Day has said that she had to learn to trust others when she moved from corporate executive to CEO: "I used to be a bright executive who majored in being right." When she took over running Lululemon, she realized that getting people to engage and take ownership wasn't about "the telling" but about letting them come into the idea in a purpose-led way. She characterized this change as the shift from "having the best idea or problem solving" to "being the best leader of people."[1]

## BECOME A DELEGATION NINJA

In recent years I have searched out and painstakingly adopted ways of managing my business and my life more efficiently and tried to give up being a perfectionist and instead embrace being an enabler of people doing their best work. While delegating used to be really hard, I know that part of being a leader is mastering this skill, no matter how much I want to be the one to make that sales call or set up a new online organization for our digital files. I now love finding new ways to do things in less time, more effectively, and with a very light touch from me. I came up with this cuff to remind me to keep it up:

I have had so many conversations with women about the tools and shortcuts I am using (Who isn't looking to free up a little time?) and pride myself on being a kind of Delegation Ninja. Don't get me wrong, this doesn't mean I think I am above doing any task, no matter how big or small. In fact there are many things I actually enjoy doing that I have to refrain from taking on because I know that it's not the best use of my time. For example, I *love* making Excel spreadsheets. I could spend hours playing with fonts and giving the columns different-colored headers and clicking on the "wrap text" function. But I don't allow myself to indulge in this pastime anymore, or not until I've done all the other things that need my attention. Mainly I have my operations manager set up these spreadsheets for me, and interns fill them in. I check them over, and sometimes, if I have a few minutes, I can put on the finishing touches.

What if we try to apply Pam's maxim that all failure can be traced back to management—which came straight out of her Harvard Executive Education program—to our lives? Instead of worrying about managing the failures, we could successfully manage our way to having more time, less stress, and a wider runway to accomplish our goals. Does that seem possible? Why is it that we working women seem totally stressed out, to indulge in a much-overused phrase, most of the time? Does it have to be that way, or have we failed to manage the most important thing we have: our own lives and minds?

Let's pause a minute and look at what women are doing with their time and why they are doing it. Why is it that women are working harder at work *and* at home? I don't know about you, but I am really tired of reading studies about how, in most relationships, women are still doing 70 to 80 percent of the housework, on top of having full-time jobs. To me, the solution is simple: we have got to become a whole lot better at delegating. Sure, men get more egalitarian with every generation and do more around the house. My husband is a genuine supporter of women and believes in sharing the duties at home. But still, he is just not going to wash fingerprint marks off walls. I am. Or I'll find someone to do it.

The risk of not learning the delegation skills is working harder but not smarter, and in some cases burning out. A report on women-owned businesses in the twenty-first century found that women have a higher likelihood of shutting down their business than men do (72 percent survival rate for male-owned compared to 66 percent for women-owned). Learning to hand off responsibility is one of the antidotes to getting to the end of your rope. It also gives you more bandwidth to focus on responsibilities you can't and shouldn't hand off, like keeping a close eye on your cash flow, and profits and losses.

If your inner perfectionist is worried about things not getting done "right," you can apply another one of Pam's great rules: "Trust, but verify." Give people room to get things done without looking over their shoulder, but do make sure to double-check the work. If the project doesn't come out the way you wanted, find a better way to explain it and take 100 percent responsibility. Chances are, if you hired the right people, they will get it right the next time. And then you can hand it off permanently.


## DOING IT ALL AND RUNNING ON EMPTY

A couple of years ago I felt I was reaching the limit of what I could handle as a working mom and business owner. Little Pim was by then a venture-backed, multimillion-dollar business with nine employees, and it demanded 90 percent of my work attention. In the other 10 percent of the time allotted for work I was teaching Double Digit Academy, serving on the advisory council of a nonprofit called Global Language Project, filling an EO board role as communications chair, and, on the personal side, running a diversity book club for parents at my son's school. All working mothers will tell you there is also a part of your brain permanently reserved for "Did I remember to confirm the playdate, or will my son be sitting alone on the steps when school gets out?"

I finally decided I had two options: (1) give up many of the things I was doing or (2) get a whole lot better at doing them all efficiently. When I took a hard look at my commitments, I decided I truly loved them all. So I set out to do option 2.

Enter Ari Meisel, a serial entrepreneur turned efficiency consultant who came to speak to my EO group. Ari asked us to consider the question "What is the 5 percent of what you do every day that you are really, really good at and *only you* can do?" Then he challenged us to think about what would happen if we outsourced or delegated the other 95 percent. Would it lead to more business, a more well-run company, the ability to go to the gym more often, additional funding? The answer is pretty much always yes to all of it. So what are we waiting for? He also said there are times of the day when we are most sharp and need to try to reorganize our schedule to make maximum use of those times. Brilliant! And so simple. I hired him as a coach to help me get more efficient, and within two months I was a changed person.

Here is an example of how I put this into practice. At that time I was still taking the kids to school several times a week. Ari helped me have a game-changing epiphany: I am a total morning person; my brain is at its sharpest between 6:00 and 10:30. That is when I have many of my big thoughts, write my columns for *Forbes* or blog for Little Pim, and push mission-critical plans forward in my business. I couldn't afford to spend those hours shuttling back and forth to school. So I asked my husband and babysitter to take over those morning commutes and scaled back to one day a week with each child. Do I miss that time with my kids? Sometimes. Do I make up for it at other times that are less brain-intensive for me? Absolutely. I am home four or five evenings a week, spend most weekends with the family, and read to the kids every night before they go to bed. I also travel very little and do extra drop-offs and pick-ups when I can.

Once I carved out those mornings for brain work or strategic meetings with Little Pim advisors, I decided to move on to other parts of my life and look at whether I was doing things at the optimal time. Doing the dishes, reviewing sales numbers, and playing Monopoly with my kids each has a best time, if I am being honest about it. I started to think about doing each activity at what I call the "Best and Brightest Time" or BBT. Now I automatically put just about everything I do through a quick BBT filter in my mind. Instead of doing the dishes after dinner when I might still have the energy to review a contract, I put off that clean up until 10:00 p.m., by which time I'll be fuzzy headed and sudsing dishes will feel like a nice brain break! Knowing that there are BBTs for just about everything allows me to prioritize and plan more easily. For example, I try to reserve mornings for mentors and advisors who are helping *me* and to take meetings where I am *giving* advice or being social during lunch or later in the day. It can be fun figuring out what you can farm out and what you will do with the time it frees up!

## David S. Rosenblatt of 1stdibs

David Rosenblatt made his name as the CEO of DoubleClick, a technology company that in 2008 sold to Google for more than $3 billion. David now runs 1stdibs, an online marketplace for furniture, fine jewelry, vintage fashion, and fine art. He also serves on the board of Twitter and as an advisor to many early-stage media and e-commerce companies (including Little Pim). David is also on the board of IAC/InterActiveCorp, a leading media and Internet company.

### What advice do you have for women learning to delegate?

Irv Grousbeck of Stanford Business School says, "You can hire people to do everything but hire people." I live by that, it's rule number 1. Another rule I have that's become a mantra is "Only do the things that only I can do," meaning that it's only in my job description to do. That's what you should spend your time on. For everything else, see rule number 1! The hardest thing for a lot of CEOs—people who, as a rule, have tremendous confidence in their own abilities—is to come to terms with what you're not as good at, and then hire people who can do those things. If I find myself doing too many things that are actually someone else's job, then I probably don't have the right person in that position.

### When should you start thinking about delegating?

It's not necessarily the best thing in the world to be a delegator when you have six employees and you need to get the second version of your product out the door. To get to $1 million in revenues, you need to be detail-oriented. Somebody needs to be on top of it, and typically that's the founder, who has the most emotional investment and understands the customer. When you are really small, it doesn't make sense to have specialization, because you couldn't afford to hire the number of people you need to get everything done. As you get bigger, each job requires specialization. You graduate from needing generalists to needing specialists. It almost mimics cell differentiation in utero: you progressively become more specialized.

**Do you see women underselling themselves in pitch meetings? Like, do they do their pitch and then tack on "Oh, and also I have this PhD from Harvard"?** You know, if I think about the number of times I have been pitched by a man—which is 90 percent of the time—I realize that most of them aren't very good at pitching either. It is not like men are great at it and women aren't. It is hard to pitch, objectively speaking. Though I will say you are right that, in general, women are much less aggressive in asking for compensation, and they tend to qualify themselves more. I bet you anything there is a woman in your office right now who has the ability to take responsibility three times greater than what she has, but you don't see it because she is in a smaller role and not asking for more. Though most of the senior women who I have worked with have not had that problem [*laughs*] and tend to be pretty darn aggressive!

## STOP SWEEPING THE BREAD CRUMBS

Home is actually a great place to start sharpening your delegation skills. Then you can move on to your office. About four years into my marriage I still felt I was doing the bulk of the cleaning in our apartment. I also realized that my husband was not out to make my life harder; he simply didn't notice most of the things I was cleaning, so he was not motivated to take better care of them. Hiring a cleaning person to come in for four to five hours twice a month was another of the best delegation things I ever did for my sanity. Spending $80 to $100 is a small price to avoid silly arguments about our sink and be able to come home to a sparkly clean apartment.

The last important piece of delegating is to use that extra time to actually do something valuable. That might be reaching out to an advisor, answering emails, reading a business book, or just putting your feet up and watching your favorite TV show and giving your brain a break if that is what you need right then.

Not all delegation requires spending money. My husband and I now have a pretty even division of household chores, and we have also taught our two boys to help us keep the home functioning. They set the table, empty the dishwasher, and do their own laundry together once a week. I am doing what I do best: spending quality time with them, showing up at (most of) the events that matter most to them, ensuring they have a top education and top-notch enrichment activities, and, of course, loving them to bits. Everything else requires job charts, teamwork, and some extra hired hands.

What does this domestic chart have to do with how you scale up your business? Learn to delegate, and you'll be surprised by how differently you spend your time and how much other people will respect your choices and step up to fill in the gaps. The parallel between delegating at home and at work was never clearer to me than when I taught Emmett, at seven years old, to pack his own lunch for school. I showed him where we kept the bread, cold cuts, vegetables, and sandwich bags. Those first few mornings I had to almost bite my fingers not to jump in and do it for him. It would have been so much faster just to do it myself! But three days later he could do it all in six minutes. He took pride in telling people he packed his own lunch. (Plus, he could add extra cookies when I wasn't looking.) And now I had a whole five minutes to apply makeup before leaving the house instead of doing it one-handed in the elevator. I try to remember that when I am delegating at work and getting frustrated that the person didn't do it exactly as I asked. It takes time to learn to pack a lunch!

My younger son, Adrian, has the job of sweeping up the crumbs under the table. I used to crawl under there myself with the whisk broom and dustpan, but it is so much more suited to a person his size, and now that is "his area" to keep clean. Let me tell you, if you keep sweeping up those crumbs rather than assigning that job, you will be on Crumb Duty for life. It's the same in our businesses. Most of us are sweeping up more crumbs than we care to admit.

I developed the first tier of my efficiency skills when I became a mom and had to juggle my kids' needs along with the demands of a growing business. But these skills were further honed when I went out to raise venture capital. This forced me to delegate large and small tasks in my business, from sales calls to running weekly meetings, because 50 percent of my time was now spent out of the office, meeting with potential investors.

In addition to being a Delegation Ninja I became a student of efficiency and started researching and using systems that could save me time and help me hand off responsibility to team members.

Another benefit of all this delegating is that my Little Pim team learned how to function well without me there, and it gave many of them a chance to take on more leadership roles. As a double payoff, their independence turned out to be one of my biggest selling points when I was raising venture capital. Investors want to see a well-functioning team, not a solopreneur with octopus arms doing everything herself.

Maybe you are thinking that delegating sounds great, but you can't afford the someone to delegate to. That is totally normal. A big part of our job as entrepreneurs is to manage the push-pull tension of a growing business. You should be constantly pushing the limits of what you can afford in terms of staff, product, and marketing to get to the next revenue level, and pulling back if you don't reach your financial goals. If you do reach your goals or exceed them, then you can bump people from part time to full time, or replace a virtual assistant with an in-person assistant. The key thing is to start putting the organizational infrastructure in place for the size you *want* to be and to free yourself up as much as possible by delegating so you can do work that is truly your best and highest use.

## VIRTUAL ASSISTANTS CAN DO VIRTUALLY EVERYTHING

If you are wondering how to start on the road to better delegation, try hiring a virtual assistant (VA) for a few hours a week. VAs are freelance administrative assistants available at a variety of companies that manage them (Zirtual, Noon Dalton, Fancy Hands, and ODesk, to name a few). They do tasks for you remotely. You do not meet them in person, you simply manage them by email or phone, and you can reserve them for as little as one hour or for a block of five, ten, or forty hours per week. Plus, you can stop at any time. The cost tends to be very reasonable, varying from $5 to $25 per hour depending on the level of English speaking and writing you need for the tasks. Some are in the United States; others are in India or the Philippines. The tasks most often delegated to a VA are administrative ones, like generating reports, leads, and database entries. Using VAs is now a common practice among entrepreneurs.

The VA I hired is based in Maine, and we have never met. At the office I have a full-time operations manager who keeps my calendar and helps me prepare for board meetings and presentations I must make. But I have tasks that I don't feel are a good use of his time that we out-source to the VA, such as entering my contacts into a database after a trade show, finding articles on children and language learning for my social media, and researching someone online ahead of an important meeting.

There is something both unsettling and very freeing about manag-ing someone you never sat in the same room with. On the one hand, you don't build the kind of relationship that you have with people you see in person. On the other hand, you can throw just about any task at them and not worry about whether it's below their pay grade or whether they will feel put out by the request. The other reason to get a VA is that it forces you to start thinking about what you can outsource. If I asked you right now what you could delegate, you would probably say very little. But when you take a hard look at how you are spending your time—and have to fill up a VA's time—you may find that this is more of a construct in your mind than a reality. The great benefit of outsourcing tasks is that once the VA has learned to do a task, you can celebrate three great wins:

1.  You never have to do the task again because someone else knows how to do it. You can just oversee it lightly, saving you a bunch of time.
2.  If anything should happen to you or your current assistant, there is a backup person who can handle things. You just bought yourself some insurance.
3.  You got that much better at delegating. Now try outsourcing some other job you never thought you could!

Here are just a few of the things I have outsourced, who does them, and how much time I saved:

**Professional**

- Researching content for my Facebook, Twitter, and LinkedIn pages (VA). Saved three to five hours per week.
- Scheduling meetings (operations manager and VA). Saved five to seven hours per week.
- Making travel plans (operations manager and VA). Saved two to three hours per month.
- First drafts of board materials (operations manager). Saved four to six hours per quarter.
- First drafts of PowerPoint presentations (operations manager). Saved one to two hours per presentation.

**Personal**

- Setting up playdates (babysitter). Saved forty-five minutes per week.
- House cleaning (cleaner). Saved six hours per month.
- Food shopping (Fresh Direct keeps my list; babysitter puts food away). Saved three hours per week.
- Drugstore shopping (Drugstore.com keeps my list). Saved three hours per month.
- Doing the kids' laundry (my kids and babysitter). Saved two hours per week.
- Setting the table, clearing the table, sweeping under the table (my kids). Saved thirty minutes per day.
- Dry cleaning drop-off (babysitter). Saved forty-five minutes per week.

Have fun summoning your own Delegation Ninja!

## YOU, BUT BETTER: YOUR EXTERNAL BRAIN

In addition to working with VAs to rescue time that can be better spent, Ari Meisel, the efficiency coach, recommends you create what he calls "an external brain" in order to free yourself from mental clutter and allow you to access information anytime, anywhere. This will give you more space to create, lead your team, and even relax. He suggests writing everything down and maintaining a note-taking system that is archived, searchable, and shareable. The "where" matters less than not keeping it in your head. Ari recommends tools like Evernote, HassleMe, and iDoneThis.

Finding the right system for you and carrying out these new ways of managing information can take a few weeks and some trial and error. One of the best things you can do is ask other CEOs who care about efficiency to recommend their favorite apps and systems, and then try them out. I've posted some of my favorites at juliapimsleur.com.When you outsource the tasks bogging you down and become a delegation ninja, you might find you have more time to work on being the leader you want to be, to play board games with your kids, to drink margaritas, or just sleep in from time to time!

## Kara Goldin of Hint Water

COURTESY OF KARA GOLDIN

A former AOL and CNN employee, Kara Goldin kicked her Diet Coke habit but found plain water boring, so in 2005, while she was pregnant with her fourth child, she took $50,000 out of her family's savings account and started a beverage company. In 2014 the company approached $50 million in retail sales.

### *Where did the idea for your company come from?*

I think the cornerstone was my own desire to get healthy. I had always thought that I was pretty healthy. After my third child was born, I wasn't feeling that great. I didn't have diabetes or obesity. I had baby weight to lose, but overall I was just really feeling like my stomach didn't feel that great. I went to a few different doctors, and nothing was coming up as an issue. I guess I've always believed that taking medicine is not the answer. I've always believed that in order to get better I need to first try and exercise and then also look at what I'm putting into my body. And eventually I realized that it might not actually be the food that I was putting into my body but all the Diet Coke. But for me drinking plain water was just super boring, and I started drinking water with some fruit in it. I looked for the product in the marketplace and it wasn't there. I went to Whole Foods and I started asking questions and tried to figure out how to launch this company.

**What did you do to ensure Hint Water would be this big successful brand as opposed to another one-off idea?**
You have to be able to find people who believe in you, whether that's family, angels, whatever it is, and you have to be thinking about that even before you get the products to the marketplace. I think a lot of companies fail because they don't have that access to capital.

**You are the CEO, and your husband is the COO. How does that work?**
Hint was my idea, and if you were to talk to Theo about this he would say that he jumped in because I started writing checks out of our joint accounts! Also he was working in medical diagnostics, and when he saw that I was launching a company that was actually helping people before they ever got to the doctor, he became very interested in it. I'm really more about the marketing, the brand, the vision, the build side of it, and Theo is much more of the dotting all the i's, crossing all the t's. He is very detailed. I am not.

**How is it with the kids? You have three?**
Four! I was pregnant when I was developing the company, which is another reason I dragged Theo with me to my initial bottling run—because I had extreme morning sickness. Our family life and our work life are all kind of one and the same, and I think some people strive to keep those things separate. I don't, and I'm okay with that. I also feel like I'm creating change that my kids can understand.

# PUTTING THE PERSON BACK
# IN YOUR PERSONAL LIFE

One evening at a swank Manhattan bar overlooking the city, I sat having drinks at an EO Ellas event with Laura, an attractive woman who wears fabulous French silk scarves and runs a $5-million-dollar-plus public-relations company. On our second martini, she confessed that she loved her business but she really wanted to have kids, a dream that seemed all but unattainable, as she was pushing forty-four and not in a relationship.

"How do you find the challenge of balancing work and family life?" she asked.

"I love being both a boss and a mom," I told her, "even though it's chaotic. Plus, I am lucky that my husband is a very hands-on parent. He does a lot of the soccer-in-the-park stuff and takes the boys to school most days, while I do more of the coordinating of family activities and educational enrichment. That leaves me more hours free to work on my business."

"Oh, I get it," Laura said. "You wanted to have kids but not do the work."

I wanted to deck her! Not do the work? I do *tons* of work for our family. The fact that a fellow woman entrepreneur would suggest that I was shirking my motherly duties because my husband spends more weekday hours with the kids than I do reveals how far we still have to go in undoing our socialization about "good moms."

To Laura's credit, she immediately apologized once she saw the horrified look on my face, and I know she didn't mean it to come out that way. But the motherhood-is-sacrifice equation is so engrained for most of us that even the women reinventing what it means to be a modern professional woman can't easily shake these old stereotypes. It's essential that we entrepreneurs innovate here and disrupt the existing models of CEO-wife and CEO-mom if we are going to have success *and* be able to enjoy it. What's the point of having our own business if we feel we must pay for this choice at home?

I'd like to suggest that as a first step we permanently retire statements like "I feel guilty when I'm at work and I feel guilty when I'm at home." I have heard so many working mothers say this, and I sometimes wondered if we weren't indulging just a tad in self-punishment. Why not embrace the choices we have made? Long before I had kids I had made a promise to myself never to say that phrase. Happily it hasn't been hard to keep that promise because I have never felt that way. I love my time at work, and I love my time at home. I feel lucky to have an amazing family *and* run a business, even with all the hair-raising, hectic parts.

## THE PERSON IN YOUR PERSONAL LIFE

It's not just working moms who have it hard. Running a business is a stressful, full-contact sport with few free hours, no matter how efficient you are. When people ask you about your personal life, you almost want to pull out your smartphone and scroll through your contacts to see if you can find this "person" they're talking about. What personal life?

Entrepreneurs tend to be driven and passionate and, at least in the first year, work almost nonstop. I know I did. But the women who are running highly successful businesses know that eventually you have to put the *person* back in your *personal life*. This is so important that there is an entire field devoted to helping people look after themselves; it's called "personal ecology."[1] Your life outside of work actually needs as much attention as your product-development pipeline. Why? Because otherwise you will either burn out, sprout weird skin conditions, or become so one-dimensional that you will alienate your friends and family even more than you already have by talking about your business all the time!

I have made it one of my top priorities to see friends regularly; I try to set aside a couple of lunches and evenings a month just for that purpose. I consider my friends to be like extended family, and seeing them always reenergizes me. It isn't easy to carve out this time, and I admit that I often suggest lunch dates with friends so that my operations person at work will coordinate it, whereas for a weekend or evening activity I am usually the one replying to the half dozen back-and-forth planning texts and emails.

Sometimes seeing friends and *not* talking about business is just what we need to stay sane. We have to remind ourselves that we work to live, not live to work. It's critical for all women—with or without children—to create work-free times when they shut off their phones, go on that date, and blow off a morning to sleep in with a new special friend. Women who are raising a family are usually obliged to cordon off some amount of time for the family so they can't just work all the time even if they wanted to. Forcing yourself to carve out nonwork time is a blessing in disguise. I have met some incredibly efficient and effective mom CEOs who have had to make it work, and so they do.

The Million Dollar Women I know have different ways to recharge and practice self-care, but they all recognize how indispensable it is to have a routine that includes regular social and physical activity, and stick to it. Heather Hiles, CEO of Pathbrite has two teenage sons and is running a fast-growing ed-tech business. She religiously goes to hot yoga or Pilates on weekends. One thing Brittany Hodak of ZinePak did to take better care of herself was to schedule time off when she returned from long trips or red-eye flights. She said she used to get off the plane and go straight into work, but now she tries to take at least a few hours for herself before diving back in. Having it blocked off in her calendar means her team knows she is unavailable, and turning that into a practice means she doesn't have to think about it—she just does it. Gretchen Rubin's book *Better Than Before* can help you find your own perfect way of forming a new positive habit.

When I return from trade shows—after many long days of windowless conference halls and travel to other cities—I take off time to get a massage and surprise Adrian by picking him up from school and taking him out for a treat. Seeing him enjoy his pain au chocolat is a treat for me too! Better yet, this year I delegated the out-of-town trade shows. I sent my sales team to the ABC Expo Juvenile Products Show in Las Vegas and let them handle it. They closed fifteen new accounts, and I loved following their adventures on our Little Pim Facebook page!

I work out three to four mornings per week and do ten minutes of meditation each morning. (I set the alarm for 5:00 to get up before the kids.) Along with a weekly yoga class I try not to miss, these activities keep me mostly balanced and help me burn off anxiety and "stress energy." Of course there are weeks when all this goes out the window for a couple days due to a deadline or big investor meeting, but I am a much better leader, mom, and person when I don't forgo these times for myself. And because they are part of my routine, I don't have to think about them, so I can focus on my company and family.

## POWERFUL AND POSED

Some women CEOs struggle with the idea that we must be bulldozers (or other b-words) if we are going to be successful. That is an old stereotype that is going the way of VHS tapes. Most women CEOs I know have one thing in common: they are grounded. Our power comes from having a strong core, not a strident voice. I have been taking yoga classes for more than ten years, and not a class goes by that I don't think about the parallels between doing yoga and leading, specifically leading as women.

Yoga class is one of the few places where it's totally normal to fail over and over. Seeing others try to stand on their heads, do Tripod Pose or Crow or other daring feats that often lead to landing on their butt encourages me to also keep risking and trying new things. I see people strengthen their core, change over time, and learn new skills. I can finally do a headstand away from the wall—but it took me seven years! The women who can do the harder poses like Bird of Paradise, where you stand on one foot while lifting the other up in the air like a flamingo, are not just the ones with the perfectly toned bodies. Anyone can learn to do really hard poses no matter what their initial abilities. And anyone can learn to fundraise or run a successful business.

Yoga is also a place to learn about leadership. Does the yoga teacher make you want to push past your limits? Does she encourage you to challenge yourself, or does she make you feel like you failed if you can't do a perfect Warrior Three pose? When you are an entrepreneur, leading your staff is one of the most important parts of your job. You can learn so much from putting yourself in situations where you are being led by a woman. Which tactics do you want to borrow or avoid?

Yoga is good at training us not to compare ourselves with others and just push our own limits. When we are asked to do poses over and over again, we are reminded that trying is often what leads to succeeding—and you can even find pleasure in the trying. When I attempt to do a headstand and feel that inevitable fear of falling and breaking my tailbone, I remind myself to lift and tweak. If I can just get my legs into the air, I can make small adjustments and get my stance to a more stable place. I don't have to be able to send my legs up perfectly on the first try and find impeccable balance. This is true in business as well, where the important thing is often to do *something*. Then you can tweak as you go.

Yoga also encourages you to ask for help from your flying buttresses, which take the form of blocks, a fellow yogi, or a teacher. A good yoga teacher will remind her class that *shavasana* (the rest pose at the end) is the most important pose of the whole class. Yoga teaches you to focus and build endurance, pushes you to master new things, and allows you to fail without shame, then relax and recuperate. I can't think of a better business curriculum.

## Heather Hiles of Pathbrite

COURTESY OF HEATHER HILES/
PHOTO BY LAUREN CREW

The education entrepreneur Heather Hiles is one of the only women profiled in these pages who went to business school, because I want to show that it's possible to be a successful entrepreneur without traditional training. So I was relieved when Heather told me that other than learning how to read financial statements, she's figured out most of what she's needed as a CEO from being out in the world. After twenty-one years in the education and workforce development arenas, she saw a void: the e-portfolio software available was insufficient for learners' needs. So she set about building RippleSend (now Pathbrite), a SaaS product that actually improves educational outcomes by letting any student create his or her own multimedia portfolio. Not only is Heather the only woman in the room—she's often the only African American.

**How does it feel to sometimes be the odd woman out in this world?**
[*Laughs*] I was talking with Megan Smith, who runs GoogleX, and she said the HBO show *Silicon Valley* wanted to go into Google to shoot some scenes. Megan said they could come in, and she purposely put women in every position, because she had noticed how usually only men appear as substantive characters in that sit-com. After they did some filming, they were like "Excuse me, do any men work here?" It gave them a little taste of their own medicine.

**Does intentional networking help with that kind of alienation?**
Yes. When you hear people talk in these panels, most of these guys make it sound like they rolled out of bed, wrote their ideas on a napkin, went for a bike ride with some VC, got funded with a couple million dollars, and came out with something worth $100 million. I'm like "Gosh, this is wonderful, but it's not my world." I need to talk to somebody who's really done it the old-fashioned way, can tell me what my board is going to say when they look at the financials. You

don't have to know everybody, but if you know the right people who will give you the real information—boy, that's good stuff.

### When did you know it was time to raise money?

I had raised some angel funding from a couple of people and put my own money in with the prototype that I had built. Once I got validation from Stanford University that they wanted me to build out the platform, I decided to raise institutional money to move from prototype to a cutting-edge, enterprise-ready platform. I began researching the best investors in my space, and simultaneously one of the top-tier VCs approached me who wound up leading my A round.

### How do you take care of yourself?

I'm a huge fan of Bikram yoga, I do a lot of meditation, and I also do Pilates for my back, so that when I'm flying I'm not killing my back. I like to be in nature, and I soak in the hot tub in my backyard. You've got to find ways to take your time and get grounded. I believe in that very, very strongly. I also think that the idea that you are going to work nine to five and have balance every day is a myth. It's more like a campaign schedule: you go all-out for periods of time, then refuel, then go back to it.

### How do you stay inspired?

It's like basketball, which I have a background in. You have to practice every day. Where you do the hard work is in practice. I stay ready to be in the game. One can always be better, but every day you practice to improve your game. It never ends, and as you play with better opponents you have to continue to improve your quality of competition. Investors are looking at two metrics: points you put on the board, and the momentum. Even if you are down in number of points, if you have momentum, you can still win the game.

## TWICE THE DAD AND HALF THE MOM

One of my friends from college is now a VC. When I called him up to interview him for this book, he told me why he thought there were so few women CEOs: "It's such a hard job! So many pressures, so many demands, and it's really isolating."

I almost burst out laughing. I wanted to say, "Try being in labor for thirty-six hours, then having a C-section, then going home to take care of an infant, a three-year-old, and a husband, while running a business." We women do "hard" just fine. It's the being good to ourselves so that we can stay fit, both mentally and physically, where we sometimes fall down.

One of my branding consultants, Judd Harner, said it best during a brainstorming session we were having about Little Pim customers: "Today's working dad feels like he is twice the dad his father was, while today's working mom feels like she is half the mom her mother was."

Judd explained that we feel like "half the mom" because, though our moms may have had jobs, they mostly didn't have all-consuming careers. In the 1960s and 1970s, when many of our moms were "working girls," women like my mom (white, middle-class women) mainly had jobs in teaching, office administration, and other flexible fields. So they were usually there when we came home from school, volunteered to be class parent, and made brownies for the bake sales. That is what their moms had done, and they were expected to do it too, so they did.

Our dads, however, were still very much stuck in the 1950s model. They were not in the delivery room, didn't change diapers, and rarely gave Mom an afternoon off. So today's dad feels like a superhero if he does a midnight feeding, takes the kids Saturday morning while Mom goes for a run, and is actually in the room when his offspring are born.

My husband, Darren, who also works full time, always wanted to be a super-involved dad, and he is. He takes the kids to school several days a week, plays sports with them on weekends, cooks once a week, and does about a third of the housework. He believes he is a fantastic father. And he is. I, on the other hand, do roughly two-thirds of the work of running our home life—cooking, arranging sitters, coordinating our schedules, setting up playdates, buying birthday presents, making art projects, and teaching reading—while fighting the feeling that I am not a good-enough mother.

In writing this book, I know I risk getting caught up in the "mommy wars": working moms versus stay-at-home moms. Let me just say I am not "for" either. But I am clearly cut out to be the former. Darren and I are doing the same juggling act as other two-working-parents households. It's hair-raising and zany, but also deeply gratifying to do work we love and show our boys what that looks like.

I consider myself a feminist and have always believed feminism at its best is about giving women choices. A study of fifty thousand adults in twenty-five countries revealed that kids of working mothers may actually have some advantages over kids with at-home moms. (Most notably, the daughters of working moms completed more years of education, were more likely to be employed, and in the U.S., earned 23 percent more than the daughters of non-working mothers.)[2] Though I love being a working mom, I fully support and admire women like my sister-in-law Robin, who decided to stay home with her three boys under the age of eight. With her top-flight education, multitasking skills, and professional résumé, she could easily be running a business or working for a Fortune 500 company. We may be different, but we love our kids with the same fervor and believe we are giving them the best life we can offer. We are both right. And we both struggle at times with our choices.

Debora Spar writes astutely in *Wonder Women* about learning to embrace our full, crazy, sometimes maddening lives as professionals and mothers: "If women want to combine motherhood with a full-time career—or a part-time career, or a deep commitment to anything outside the nuclear family—then they need to anticipate a truly extended period of permanent chaos."[3] I know that feeling of chaos well! When it becomes too much, I remind myself that having a demanding job running a company I love *and* wanting to find time to make Emmett's favorite dinner or watch movies with my kids on the couch is a really awesome, First World, 1 percent problem to have. I try to embrace the "too muchness" and remember that chaos is a normal by-product of living such a full life.

All the way back to *Little House on the Prairie* times and even before, women have had it hard, period. At least our twenty-first-century version of hard includes a chance to build something lasting and wealth-generating, while showing our kids a powerful role model of a mom who loves what she does. My entrepreneur friend Carrie, mother to two girls under ten, says, "I pick the moments that matter to me." For Carrie, it's putting her kids to bed every night, leading their Brownie troop, and making their Halloween costumes by hand, then reconciling herself to the fact that she doesn't do drop-off or the PTA.

A candid conversation I had with my mother-in-law helped me overcome any lingering guilt I may have had about being a working mother. Susan was a stay-at-home mom and was to me the symbol of what I imagined I should be but wasn't. *She would have been on the playground bench when he skinned his knee,* I would tell myself. *She would have volunteered to run the class art project.* But one day that changed.

When my first son was still in diapers and I was juggling sitters and serving store-bought food for dinner, my mother-in-law confided in me that while she's glad she was home with her kids when they were young, she sometimes felt adrift during those years. She told me she sometimes wishes she'd pursued a career when her kids were young instead of putting hers on pause. Once the kids were grown and out of the house, she got a job working for the California state government and now runs a successful consultancy placing seniors into the right elder care facilities. My mother-in-law fully supports my entrepreneurial efforts and less hands-on style of motherhood. And she never misses a chance to tell me how amazing the boys are turning out, and "Whatever you are doing is working!" What she told me about her own struggles as a stay-at-home mom meant so much to me. It was a reminder that mothers have always had to make tough trade-offs when raising kids. Mine are no more challenging than hers were, just different.

Spar has spent years discussing women's issues at institutions like Harvard and Barnard and comparing notes with other professional women at large corporations and who own their own business. What she heard from each of them was more alike than different. Women at the top, in every industry, are still pioneers, though women have been in the workforce in large numbers since the 1940s. And we are all trying to figure out how to make it all work, with varying degrees of success and pull-our-hair-out frustration, depending on the day.

I can have weeks at a time when I feel so overjoyed to have my full-to-the-brim existence, with work I love and two boys who are the lights of my life. But then my sitter cancels or a board member needs to speak with me urgently, and I curse my inability to be in two places at once. I remember some of the best advice my mother ever gave me: "You can have it all. Just not all at once."

What if we flip the cliché "I am not giving my best at work or at home because I am always pulled between the two?" What if we instead train ourselves to recognize that what we have is the opposite: an embarrassment of riches that no woman in history prior to this time could have imagined for herself?

## WHAT DO I WANT MOST?

Making these judgment calls about what we want most is not easy. I'll never forget the time I took an important call from a board member on my cell phone while sprinting for kindergarten pick-up on a day I told Adrian I would be there. I arrived ten minutes late and found my son in tears. He ran into my arms, burying his sweet little head into my neck, and cried pitifully, "I was the only one left! All the other moms were here!" I felt like the worst mom in the world. While Adrian blew his nose on my shoulder, I saw out of the corner of my eye a stay-at-home mom—who, by the way, used to be a top-flight lawyer—sharing a carefully prepared snack of carrots and hummus with her daughter.

Those moments of tough choices and negative self-comparison to the choices other women make are never going to be fully behind me, but over time I've developed some tricks for merging home and work and staying more or less sane while doing so. I am no relationship or family expert and I only share these experiences to let you know that we all live with these contradictions. We know we are fortunate to have so many things we love and people who need us, but this fullness can sometimes feel untenable. I also find it helpful to remember that no one "has it all"—not men, not women, not kids. We all get some things we want and not others. When faced with any tug-of-war between work and home, I have learned to ask myself, "What do I want most?"

I have to make this call on a daily basis. Sometimes I opt to go to the business conference. Sometimes I stay home and build Lego towers with Adrian. There are a lot of factors at work in every decision, but in every case I focus the issue by asking what I want most in that instance and what will matter the most and to whom. If Adrian really needs my attention and it's a morning when I can write the blog post or board memo from home, then I will choose to go in late. But if I have an investor meeting, my sitter will have to make the chicken soup for a child who has a fever.

This summer Adrian, my six-year-old, was learning to ride a bicycle and I really wanted to be there when he took his first spin around the playground without training wheels. But I also really wanted this book you're holding to be written before school started, so I let my husband be the one to go to the park with him on weekends. Then one day, he did it! Darren told me how Adrian shrieked with glee as he took his first two-wheeled joy ride. For a moment I felt so deflated and sad to have missed that special moment, but I reminded myself that I had spent months teaching him to swim and had helped him learn to read and that we do fun baking projects together all year round. And I made my Labor Day manuscript deadline, for which my sons both said they were proud of me—as I am of Adrian, who is now a speed demon on that bike.

If you don't want to make those tough choices, then you need to know that about yourself and set your sights accordingly. You can also train yourself to move out of victim-like thinking into a take-charge-and-fix-it way of thinking. A few years ago when Darren and I were looking for tools to get through a rough patch, we attended a couples workshop where we learned about "taking 100 percent responsibility." This simply means that when you are not happy with your partner's behavior you need to ask yourself, "What might be different if I took 100 percent responsibility for the situation instead of blaming my partner?" It's a pretty radical tool for shifting your perspective.

We might need a little help figuring out how to take 100 percent responsibility. I know I did. I spent years mildly resenting how busy and stretched thin I was, but one day I tried out the 100 percent responsibility on my own life and realized I had chosen to have two big jobs, CEO and mom, and had best embrace it. That means realizing that I opted for a life where I sometimes wind up staring at a clock in an important meeting, praying it will wrap up in time for a parent-teacher conference or curriculum night.

What does taking 100 percent responsibility look like in a relationship? It usually means resisting the easier route of stopping at feeling hurt, and proactively taking steps to make things better. While writing this book, I was feeling a bit far from Darren, my husband of twelve years, and I had to dust off the 100 percent responsibility training from our couples retreat. I thought about a conversation I had with a married boss of mine when I was in my twenties. We were working on a film together, and in between editing notes one day she told me that she and her husband were "having a bad year." At the time, as a single person in New York whose romantic partners rarely lasted past the thrill of courting, the idea of an entire *year* of things not being good sounded like an unbearable sentence. But of course now that I am married I realize that you can have a bad stretch. And yes, it can even last a whole month or a whole year!

In our case, it had been a tough few weeks heading into fall. This was a very busy back-to-school, complicated by our older son, Emmett, being on a soccer team that had practices and games three to four times a week and by my finishing this book. Darren's organization had doubled in size, and he was needed at work on weekends and on more weeknights than ever. I started feeling a bit like we weren't connected or really following each other's lives in a meaningful way and started to grow resentful that he wasn't making more of an effort to schedule a nice dinner or suggest a movie date. I could feel myself starting to stew about his lack of attention, and when I did see him we got into silly spats about real things like whether to have friends over and ridiculous things like why *my* clothes were drying on *his* towel rack.

One Monday morning I woke up feeling especially lousy, and the only word I could think of was *estranged*, despite our sharing a bed and two amazing boys. During my morning run I was dwelling on the things Darren had done to hurt my feelings over the weekend and was a bit relieved that he was out when I got home so I could have the apartment to myself. When I got to the office, I learned that my lunch date had canceled. My lunch slots are usually booked three weeks in advance, so this was a windfall. Before I filled up that time with something else, the 100 percent rule bubbled up and made a loud virtual popping sound. *What would I be doing right now if I took 100 percent responsibility for making things better with Darren?* I asked myself. Probably not sulking. I shot off a quick text to my husband: "Free for lunch? I'd love to come to your office and take you out." He often doesn't get back to texts for a few hours, but this time he wrote right back: "Sounds great!" I immediately felt a sense of well-being wash over me. At that lunch we finally had a chance to remember why we enjoy spending time together and why we are more than two adults comanaging a high-functioning kids' club.

When my friend Debbie, also an entrepreneur, called me recently to ask for advice, I helped her use a combination of 100 percent responsibility and "What do you want most?" to make a crucial decision. The lease was up on her children's clothing store, and she was on the fence about whether to renew it for another five years. She didn't mind the long hours when her kids were babies, but now that they were five and seven she missed spending time with them. Her youngest had recently started asking her why she wasn't home after school when he got back, and it was gnawing at her. She found herself feeling jealous of her babysitter and the adventures she had with the boys while Debbie was at work. What she wanted most was to be with her children. She decided not to renew the lease, even though it was a hard and emotionally challenging decision. We also talked about the fact that she could always start her store back up again somewhere else or find a job with more freedom that would value her entrepreneurial background.

## MAKING YOUR BUSINESS PART OF THE FAMILY STORY

I was working a lot at Little Pim when my first son was in his preschool years. While I sometimes wondered if he wasn't getting enough of my time, I also tried to involve him as much as possible—bringing him on video shoots, asking for his opinion when making creative choices, and enlisting his help when I checked the subtitles on our DVDs. One night at a family dinner when Emmett was about three and a half, he said to his father, "*You* work with the Community Project," my husband's employer. Then he gestured to me in an inclusive way and said, "And Mom and I do Little Pim!" I was overjoyed to hear that he thought of it as "our" company and took pride in what "we" did!

At a certain point in my career I wanted most to make social issues documentaries. I wanted it more than money, more than stability, and more than having a steady relationship. When I hit my early thirties, however, I looked around at the women ten years ahead of me and found that very few had families or were in long-term relationships. I had to do some tough refiguring. I knew I wanted very much to have a life partner and children, and I didn't see that happening with the career I was in, where I mainly dated itinerant camera people who were dreaming of filming in faraway places, not starting a family.

It was a wrenching decision, but after five years of running my film production company (called Big Mouth Productions, for all the brassy women who worked with my partner Katy and me), I took 100 percent responsibility and chose to leave. Katy took over the company, and I became a full-time fundraiser instead of a filmmaker. I liked to joke that I went from being the person everyone wanted to talk to at a party (as a filmmaker) to the person you'd walk away from (as a fundraiser). But for me, it was the right decision. Coincidentally or not, I met my husband around that time. We were married a year later, and we had our first son two years after that.

You can take the woman out of the company, but apparently you can't take the company out of the woman, because while on maternity leave I came up with the idea for Little Pim and, bam, I had a company again.

Not all women are or want to be married or with a life partner, and I don't subscribe to the idea that you have to have a supportive partner to be able to raise kids and run a company. I know women who are extremely career-driven and whose husbands hardly help at all, and single mothers who are killing it in business. They solve this by working close to home, hiring more full-time care, or turning to their parents if that is an option. There is always a way to create more time once you take 100 percent responsibility, ask what you want most, and are prepared to act on it. Samantha Razook, CEO of Curious Jane camps for girls, describes her life like this: "I get up every morning completely jazzed about going to work. I have two girls, a fourth grader and a seventh grader, and I'm divorced. . . . I have all these different calendars I'm juggling on my phone and I'm doing five thousand things, and I love it all!"

Whenever I find myself drifting into Bosszilla, overworked and over-stressed, I remind myself that the goal isn't just running a business that works: it's running a business that *works for me*. Otherwise what is the point? I could go work for a large company and run a division and have a matching 401k and never have to futz with tech at my slideshow presentations. That sounds pretty good sometimes! But I also know I would have a very hard time working for someone.

So I embrace the contradictions and try to take that extra yoga class or leave early every so often and sink into a comfy chair for a pedicure. Then I hurry home and make dinner, check homework, answer emails, and remember to feel grateful. I truly believe the greatest gift we can give to the next generation of working women is these three words: *Lose the guilt.* When we do, we realize how lucky we are to have this particular set of problems: having too many things we love to do.

## Sharon Hadary

The founding and former executive director of the Center for Women's Business Research and coauthor of the book *How Women Lead*, Sharon Hadary is a leading expert in the field of women and entrepreneurship.

***If you could change anything about women's thinking, what would it be?***
If I had only one thing to change for women it would be to encourage them to think big from the first day they start their business. Because if you think big when you start, you will establish the infrastructure to collect data on performance, finance, sales, and so on. This is the information you need to build your business successfully. It also means that three to five years after you started the business, when you are ready to go to the bank for loans or to go out for external investment, you will have the data that the banks or the investors are looking for to show growth.

**What kind of self-limiting beliefs do you hear from women?**

I was just talking with a woman getting an MBA and she was fretting about how she felt she was not comfortable with math. This is a fear many women express. The most successful business women tell me it's not about knowing how to add numbers. It's about what numbers tell you about trends, the health of the business, and where you need to make corrections. It's learning what story your numbers tell. I remember one woman business owner who often gave expert testimony about financials. One day the judge said to her, "What makes you an expert? Anybody can add numbers," and she said, "Yes, but I know which numbers to add."

# CONCLUSION

# WOMEN IN MOTION
# STAY IN MOTION

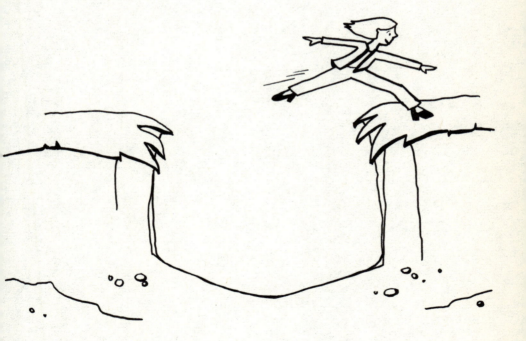

J ack Welch, business coach and former chairman and CEO of GE, says about entrepreneurs, "The best thing about entrepreneurs is their optimism. And the worst thing about entrepreneurs is their optimism!"[1] We often put spin on the spin, but this *really is* the best time there has ever been for women entrepreneurs to take their businesses big. We have opportunities to raise capital, find our flying buttresses, and run businesses that work for us that my great-grandmother Ada, running her cigarette and candy store, could never have dreamed possible. Women entrepreneurs have an unprecedented shot at the good life—or at least the good life for driven, hardworking women who are determined to find a way.

I am not minimizing the real challenges we all face. But we can overcome these challenges and be trailblazers for future generations of women entrepreneurs. We finally have some tailwind after so many years of headwind! There are more institutional and angel investors actively looking to invest in capable women leaders than ever before. Venture capital investment reached its highest level in a decade in 2014 and there are more and more women angels investing in other women.[2]

Now we just need to have the right mindset and skill set and teach one another the dance. I can finally read stories almost every day about successful women entrepreneurs in *Forbes*, the *Wall Street Journal*, and other business journals. We are making dosh *and* making significant contributions to our local economies as employers and taxpayers. We are contributing to the global economy as a collective force—and the world is paying attention.

Check out this stat: if women-owned businesses in the U.S. had their own country, we would have the fifth largest GDP (gross domestic product) in the world, just behind Germany and ahead of France and the United Kingdom.[3] Though the number of million-dollar businesses in the U.S. is still tiny, the number of women-owned companies making over $10 million in revenues grew by a whopping 57 percent over a recent ten-year period.[4] As we scale up our businesses and encourage other women to pursue their own entrepreneurial dreams, we will add another 500,000 jobs to the U.S. economy in the next decade. More and more women *are* figuring out how to go big, and millions more will join them.

One great indicator of progress is the sheer number of women starting businesses. According to a study from Babson College's Center for Entrepreneurship, one out of every ten women in the United States is becoming an entrepreneur.[5] Then there is the number of awards and summits for entrepreneurial women, such as the Brava! Award for women CEOs and the EY Entrepreneurial Winning Women Award. There are also increasing numbers of women starting tech companies, one of the last holdouts of male-dominated industries. Google recently announced that they are giving $1 million to forty partner organizations in order to help increase the representation of women in tech communities across the globe.[6] They explained in their press release that they are championing women in part because they know "women-led tech companies achieve 35 percent higher return on investment, and, when venture-backed, bring in 12 percent more revenue than male-owned tech companies."[7] Investing in women in tech will become more and more attractive, and investors will seek to back women CEOs who are yielding high returns.

## WOMEN AT THE TOP = POSITIVE ROI

When I recently visited Yale for an alumni reunion weekend, I was delighted to see a new monument called *The Women's Table*. As an undergraduate I had been keenly aware that of the forty statues on campus, not one was of a woman. *The Women's Table*, designed by the Yale grad Maya Lin, creator of the Vietnam War Memorial in Washington, D.C., now sits right in front of the main library. Engraved in this six-foot round table made of elegant granite is a series of numbers that show how many female students have attended Yale since it was founded as an all-male college in 1701. The inviting table has become a place women come to kick off women-centered celebrations and where alumnae can reflect on how relatively recently we have had a presence. For the year 1969, the number engraved on the table is 499. By 1995 there were 5,225 women at Yale. The number of women multiplied tenfold in two decades and graduating classes today are 50 percent female or more. If a three-hundred-year-old traditionally all-male bastion like Yale can make space for women, so can the Rock Dudes, the professional organizations we join, and the business world at large.

Now is our time to create thriving, scalable businesses that give us financial and personal freedom. This doesn't always require raising money, but I hope I've convinced you that it often does if it can help you get farther faster, and bring you new champions and partners.

When you cross the milestone of $1 million in annual revenues, you will find one of the clearest routes to the ultimate goal: the Triple Win of Money, Meaning, and Mobility. I still feel giddy with gratitude twice a day: when I walk into my office and am greeted by my fantastic staff, and when I walk back into my apartment and my boys run to me and say, "Mom, you're home!"

When Little Pim passed the $1 million mark, I had a strong team in place, including investors, staff, and advisors, who are as dedicated as I am to ensuring the company thrives. With this kind of support, new choices became available. I can remain CEO or move to a different role; I can sell the company or raise funds for new initiatives. I can lead workshops and write this book and help other women get ahead.

Isaac Newton's first law of physics is "Objects in motion stay in motion." What we need to do more than anything is to get in motion on raising capital, learning to delegate, knowing our numbers, and doing intentional networking. Then we can fill in any other skills gaps with books like Verne Harnish's *Scaling Up* and programs like EO Accelerator. There are so many things you'll need to know to run a successful business that I could not possibly cover them all in this book. Just to name a few: negotiating contracts, managing your financials, knowing your leadership style, creating your company's core values, and making great hires. But by reading *Million Dollar Women*, you have gotten into motion. By doing some of the exercises and reading the books mentioned, you will be giant steps ahead. Then, as I like to say, have the fear, and keep going anyway!

If you ever need a little inspiration, just think of Denise Wilson, an oboist who started building her private jet company after Googling "how to start a business." Now she has more than thirty jets and is on track to make $20 million this year. Or Heather Hiles, CEO of Pathbrite, who went from scoring points on the basketball court to scoring millions of dollars for her company and developing game-changing education software.

When someone tries to undermine you, channel your inner Brittany Hodak, who said from the very start, even when her company wasn't worth anything yet, "This is a one hundred million dollar business" and was able to laugh off people who asked her, "But who *really* owns the company?" She got going and figured it out along the way. We are all doing something brave, ambitious, and groundbreaking, even though some days it feels like we are on our way down on a bungee jump. As Diane von Furstenberg says, "We all have a Wonder Woman inside us."[8] So grab one of my Wonder Woman cuffs and benefit from mantras that have helped other women entrepreneurs. Consider sharing your own mantras at juliapimsleur.com. I want to know what gets you farther faster, and so do other women reading this book.

One of the business leaders I interviewed summed up his view of the difference between men and women CEOs: "Men need for there to be a loser to feel like they have won. If there isn't someone lying on the field, it isn't a victory. It seems to me that women think they can win, and so can other women. That, to me, is one of the best things women have going for them."

I couldn't agree more. Every day I meet CEOs running successful businesses who are eager to help, and more and more women are stepping up as mentors, investors, and advisors helping women find an easier way forward. I can also testify from my research that in addition to amazing Million Dollar Women like the ones whose stories I shared here, we have plenty of top-performing CEOs who are men cheering us on. Millions of men too are actively mentoring women in their offices, families, social circles, and professional organizations. So let's get to success the "female way." Let's build businesses that work for us, and then let's meet up and share best practices and laugh about the crying-on-the-couch moments, because we all have those too.

To my great joy, my first Little Pim employee, Stacey Brook, mentioned several times in this book, became an entrepreneur three years ago. She is the CEO of College Essay Advisors, a fast-growing company that helps kids ace their college essays. She recently told me, "Watching you build everything from scratch made me think I could do it too." One of our social media marketers, Jana, who learned to do online marketing while at Little Pim, also started her own company, to connect bloggers and brands via social media marketing. She was able to take it with her when she moved with her husband to London. That's one of the mobility advantages I am talking about.

I want to help Stacey, Jana, my fifty Double Digit Academy graduates, and one million women get to the $1-million-in-revenues mark by 2020. Together we will rewrite what it means to be a CEO. What will that look like? It will look like the women profiled in this book, who work hard for themselves and for their families rather than for a boss. They work how they choose and when they choose. They work at something that they love. And they stand to win big. Even though they're under tremendous pressure, trying to lead while learning about liquidation preferences, getting ready for a date, and checking homework, it mostly doesn't feel like work at all. Because it's theirs. And it can be yours too.

I told you that I almost shut down my business but instead went far out of my comfort zone to find a way forward. I was staring down that twenty-foot chasm and had to figure out a new way across. What is your chasm, and how are you going to get to the other side? Gina Mollicone-Long likes to say that to succeed, you have to do more than give it everything you've got. You have to give it what it takes.

As you look for the catapult to get across your chasm, remember my favorite cuff: "Fortune favors the brave." I know you too will find a way—by leaning on your peeps, discovering the scalable part of your business, filling up your mini-storage vault, and finding the right people to invest in your company's most valuable asset: you.

See you on the other side!

# ACKNOWLEDGMENTS

This book is the result of hundreds of conversations, blogs and articles exchanged, coffee dates, coaching sessions, and moments that moved me so deeply I wanted to write this book when I really didn't have time to do it. I wrote the first draft in the summer of 2014 over a thirty-seven-day period when I got up every morning at 5:00 a.m. and wrote until 7:00 before going to work.

I want to thank James Melcher for believing in me. I want to thank my coaches, Ari Meisel, Gina Mollicone-Long, Steve Nakisher, and Bill Smartt, for the skills and the roadmap to get out of my own way. I have had tremendously generous and wise advisors and mentors over the years: Stuart Farr, Carolyn Fikke, Corey Kupfer, Josh Reibel, Tom Rothman, Shep Sepaniak, and Pam Wolf. My peers who helped me through umpteen challenges and celebrated the wins deserve a huge shout-out: Joe Apfelbaum, Jenny Argie, Christel Caputo, Sarah Endline, Sam diGennaro, Mitchell Goss, Carrie Kerpen, Richard Levychin, Ryan Payne, Matt Schwartz, Nick Tarascio, Jonathan Teller, and everyone who ever answered one of my "Can you help?" emails. Special thanks to ally and pal David Sze at Greylock Partners. Debora Spar at Barnard College gave me a significant boost by reading chapters. My board, advisors, and investors, you are all part of every Little Pim success, and I am so grateful to have you in my inner circle. Paul Greenberg, you encouraged me to go big with this book, and that one conversation while running along the Hudson changed everything.

My friends in the Entrepreneurs' Organization and in EO Accelerator have listened, encouraged, read drafts, made me laugh, let me take selfies with them, and basically kept me sane. I really can't imagine doing any of this without you all having my back! The EO Board is a group of outstanding human beings I adore and admire, and my EO Accelerator Board are phenomenal leaders who have inspired and buoyed me.

The Double Digit Academy has had its own guardian angels: Melanie Schnoll-Begun, Oscar Cantu, and Mitchell Rock at Morgan Stanley, Kim Fields at Insperity, and Stefanie Syman and Heather Myers at Spark No. 9. To all the women who graduated Double Digit Academy, your courage and passion inspired this book. To the Million Dollar Women Brain Trust—my Wonder Women entrepreneurial sisters—you put so much wind in my sails and were with me every step of the way. The women entrepreneurs and business leaders I interviewed for this book were so eloquent and generous. Thank you for letting me share your stories.

*Million Dollar Women* benefited from the research of my tireless and brilliant advisor Adam Quinton, who read multiple drafts; the generous and committed Amanda Brown at the National Women's Business Council; my talented researcher Jorie Feldman; and my writing sister-in-arms, Ada Calhoun. Huge thank-you to Heather Willems for giving us million-dollar artwork!

I had a fantastic editor, Priscilla Painton, who knew when to ask for more and when to cheerlead. *Je te remercie du fond de mon cœur.* I have the most supportive and smart agent I could imagine, Zoë Pagnamenta ("Just keep swimming"), and Jayme Johnson and her team at Worthy Marketing have made navigating brandbuilding do-able and even delightful. I also owe a huge heartfelt thanks to Sophia Jimenez and the fantastic marketing, publicity, and design women at Simon & Schuster.

My Little Pim staff, you are worth every second of every pitch I made to potential investors, even the ones who referred to women as "girls." Thank you, Christina Henricks—one day you will run anything you want! Then I hope you will have a you. I adore my Little Pim family (present and past) and owe the success of our company to the fantastic people who brought their talents to our West 14th and West 17th Street offices. Alyson Shapero = best copilot ever. Period.

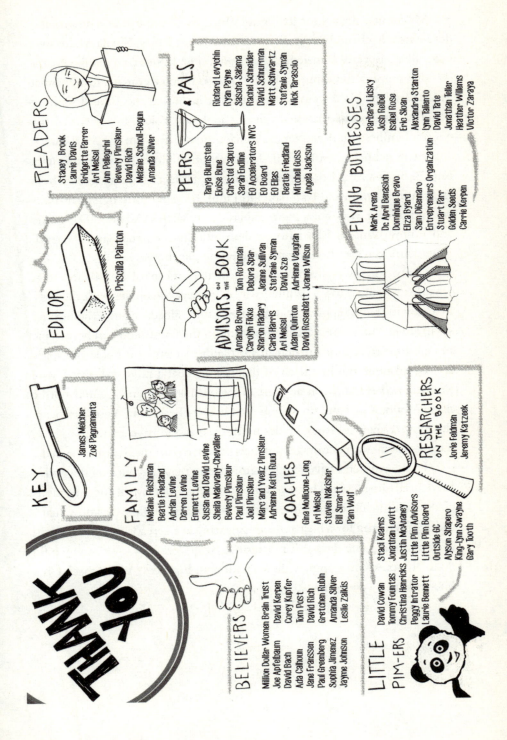

# THANK YOU

## KEY
James Melcher
Zoë Pagnamenta

## EDITOR
Priscilla Painton

## READERS
Stacey Brook
Laurie Davis
Bridgette Farrer
Ari Meisel
Ann Pellegrini
Beverly Pimsleur
David Rich
Melanie Schnoll-Begun
Amanda Silver

## PEERS & PALS
Tanya Blumstein
Eloise Bune
Christel Caputo
Sarah Endline
EO Accelerators NYC
EO Board
EO Elias
Beatie Friedland
Mitchell Goss
Angela Jackson
Richard Levyoohin
Ryan Payne
Sascha Salama
Rachel Schneider
David Schnurman
Matt Schwartz
Stefanie Syman
Nick TaraScio

## ADVISORS on the BOOK
Amanda Brown
Carolyn Fikke
Sharon Hadary
Carla Harris
Ari Meisel
Adam Quinton
David Rosenblatt
Tom Rothman
Debora Spar
Jeanne Sullivan
Stefanie Syman
David Sze
Adrienne Vaughan
Joanne Wilson

## FLYING BUTTRESSES
Mark Arena
Dr. April Benasich
Dominique Bravo
Eliza Byard
Sam DiGennaro
Entrepreneurs Organization
Stuart Parr
Golden Seeds
Carrie Kerpen
Barbara Lidsky
Josh Reibel
Isabel Rose
Eric Sloan
Alexandra Stanton
Lynn Taliento
David Tate
Jonathan Teller
Heather Williams
Victor Zaraya

## FAMILY
Melanie Fleischman
Beatie Friedland
Adrian Levine
Darren Levine
Emmett Levine
Susan and David Levine
Sheila Malovany-Chevallier
Beverly Pimsleur
Paul Pimsleur
Joel Pimsleur
Marc and Yveliz Pimsleur
Adrienne Keith Ruud

## COACHES
Gina Mollicone-Long
Ari Meisel
Steven Nakisher
Bill Smartt
Pam Wolf

## RESEARCHERS on the BOOK
Jorie Feldman
Jeremy Katzeek

## BELIEVERS
Million Dollar Women Brain Trust
Joe Apfelbaum
David Bach
Ada Calhoun
Jane Franssen
Paul Greenberg
Sophia Jimenez
Jayme Johnson
David Cowan
David Kerpen
Corey Kupfer
Tom Post
David Rich
Gretchen Rubin
Amanda Silver
Leslie Zaikis

## LITTLE PIM-ERS
David Cowan
Tommy Fountas
Christina Henricks
Peggy Intrator
Laurie Bennett
Staci Kearns
Jonathan Levitt
Justin McAnaney
Little Pim Advisors
Little Pim Board
Outside GC
Alyson Shapero
King-Lynn Swayne
Gary Tooth

My family, thanks for loving me through all the ups and downs and desperates: Melanie Fleishman, Adrienne Keith Ruud, Sheila Malovany-Chevallier, Beverly Pimsleur, Marc and Yveliz Pimsleur—thank you for all your support and care packages. I owe so much to the institutions that invested in me via generous scholarships, including the Ethical Culture Schools, the French National Film School, and Yale University. To my chosen families and dear friends, you are the reason I can fly: Mark Arena and Jason Arbuckle, Dominique Bravo and Eric Sloan, Tanya Blumstein, Kara Bobroff, Claire Boulanger, Eliza Byard and Eva Kolodner, Katy Chevigny, Paul Franklin and Jean Paul Florentin, Kirsten Johnson, Amanda Silver and Jeremy Horowitz, Lynn Taliento and Michael Warren, Dave Tate and Jimmy Canton, Isabel Rose, Alexandra Stanton, and Sam Natapoff. Ann, thank you for choosing me and letting me choose you.

Mom, you always told me I was a writer and that I could succeed at whatever I wanted to do. While I wrote, you baked cookies with the kids, helped with book reports, read my drafts, and talked through the big and small issues. Adrienne, you are the writer in the family and you helped me be one too from your kitchen in Portland. Darren, you made the space so I could write the first draft of this book. What a huge gift, thank you. Emmett and Adrian, you are part of everything I do and I could not be more proud of you and the young men you are becoming. You already are the most thoughtful Rock Dudes on the planet and have so much to give. Thanks for all the encouragement and patience with me. It really helped.

To the women I have met, mentored, and marched with on the entrepreneurial journey, this book is a tribute to your hard work and ambitious goals. I will be cheering you on while you climb, and please know that I too am preparing for a board meeting, staring at a spreadsheet, pitching an investor, and some days just muttering, "If it were easy, everyone would do it." If you see me, come tell me about your business. As my coach Gina once told me, I *am* you.

# MILLION DOLLAR WOMEN EXERCISES

Your invisible jet awaits you! Climb in and floor it. Doing these exercises will help you become a Million Dollar Woman faster. They're also a great springboard for working with an accountability partner or mentor. You can write down your answers here, or download the exercises at juliapimsleur.com.

## CHAPTER 1: HOW I GOT OFF THE ENTREPRENEUR'S HAMSTER WHEEL

1. Dream big. How can you determine whether your business can grow, generate more revenue, and be more scalable than it is today? Write down three people with whom you can talk this through. Think of friends who are successful entrepreneurs, a former professor, coaches, advisors, or mentors. Make a date and ask them to help you imagine the turbocharged version of what you are doing now.

Example:

Harrison Foster                          2/19 at 9 a.m.

Name                                     Date/Time of Meeting

_____               _____

_____               _____

_____               _____

2.  Learn from what has worked. What are some of the most successful businesses in your space, and how did they scale up? I looked at case studies of successful toy and entertainment companies before I launched Little Pim. Are there companies you can research that do something similar to what you do or have a similar model? What can you learn from how they grew their customer base and revenues? Name three successful companies in your space and start Googling. Describe their model (the short version) here and keep the fuller version on file to refer back to and share with people helping you grow your business.

Example:

Plum Organic built a well-regarded brand in the baby food category, with a key differentiator being its organic content. They focused on branding and wide distribution in their first few years and ultimately partnered with an operations group to help them scale their operations.

a.  _____

model:  _____

_____

_____

_____

b.  _____

model:  _____

_____

_____

c. _____

model: _____

_____

_____

3. What is your twenty-foot chasm, and how are you going to cross it? Are there things you are doing in your business that you are pretty sure you need to change in order to go to the next level? If yes, what are they? List three things here.

    Example:

    My twenty-foot chasm: I want to franchise my business.

    To get across: I need to learn how the franchise model works and attend franchise trade shows to meet industry contacts.

    Or

    My twenty-foot chasm: I want to be the leader in my field, PR.

    To get across: Become a thought leader by doing more blogging, social media, and public speaking, do more networking, have a scalable product I sell in addition to my other services.

a. _____

b. _____

c. _____

## CHAPTER 2: POWERFUL AND PREPARED, NOT PRETTY AND PERFECT

1. What are your top three limiting beliefs about yourself as a business person? The first step in getting rid of these beliefs is to name them. Right away this takes some of the power out of them. Then you can get to work on finding a storage plan!

Example:

I won't be able to raise money because I can't speak "finances."

No one in my family has ever run a business, so how can I?

a. _____

b. _____

c. _____

2. Write each sentence again, affirming that you are the opposite of those beliefs. Now that you have seen how your beliefs look on paper (not as powerful as they were in your head, huh?), try to add "not yet" to the ends of these statements.

Example:

I make investors feel comfortable with my command of the financials.

I have the skills I need in order to be a successful leader and CEO.

a. _____

b. _____

c. _____

3. Which are your top priorities for change? Use the space below to think about which top three skills you need to get closer to the positive opposite of your limiting beliefs.

Example:

Gain confidence in my ability to manage a sales team.

Improve my negotiating skills.

a. _____

b. _____

c. _____

4.  If you put your limiting beliefs in mini-storage, what would you make room for?

    Example:

    Creating a three-year plan for my business.

    Doing more public speaking, becoming more of a thought
      leader in my field.

    a.  _____
    b.  _____
    c.  _____

5.  Who can help you achieve your goals for growth?

    Example:

    My friend/family member who is an entrepreneur.

    My former boss.

    a.  _____
    b.  _____
    c.  _____

6.  What is something you feel you failed at in your professional or personal life, and what strength did it give you?

    Example:

    I launched a business called Script Source and it failed. This
    gave me the understanding that I can fail and still keep my
    friends, my pride, and my sense of self.

    _____
    _____
    _____
    _____
    _____

## CHAPTER 3: IDENTIFY YOUR ALLIES, YOUR FOES, AND YOUR FRENEMIES

1. Who are the friends you can count on to cheerlead as you seek to grow your company and learn new skills? Who should you move up your social priority list?

   a. _____

   b. _____

   c. _____

2. Who are the frenemies you need to find a new way of spending time with that doesn't involve discussing your business because it's just too demoralizing?

   a. _____

   b. _____

   c. _____

3. Who needs to get moved down your social list if you are going to go big?

   a. _____

   b. _____

   c. _____

## CHAPTER 4: BE LIKE NOTRE DAME, NOT THE EIFFEL TOWER

1. Find your flying buttresses. Make a chart that shows the areas of your business where you need help and whether you think an advisor or paid coach is the right solution. Some common categories are listed below. Fill in the blanks with your business needs and where you might find the help.

## Sample Buttresses Chart

| Business Need | Where to Find | Buttress |
|---|---|---|
| Accounting/Finance | Banking, Private wealth manager, CFO | Jill, my aunt's friend who was head of Private Wealth Management at UBS for 10 years and recently retired. |
| Distribution (Mass Retail) | Entrepreneur or former entrepreneur, Buyer from a large company with mass retail distribution experience | Elizabeth, former professor who taught entrepreneur class. Rob, who went to a top business school— one of his friends? |
| Managing sales people | Former entrepreneur, head of sales in a large company | Jane, sales coach, met at networking event |

2. List three people who are already helping you, even if it's just informally, and can potentially serve as one of your advisors or connect you to someone in their network.

   Example:

   Gail, lawyer at big firm, whom I often call when I get an important contract to ask her to look it over.

   a. _____

   b. _____

   c. _____

3. Craft an email to existing advisors to ask them to be an official advisor. Once they have accepted, ask them to connect you to others so you can build your advisory council.

   Sample email (insert your own info in the brackets):

*Dear [Francesca],*

*Thanks again for all you have done to help me build [Little Pim]. When you coached me through negotiating the deal with [Magna Distribution] last January, it made all the difference. I know I have much more favorable terms because of all the time you spent with me.*

*I am writing to ask you to consider joining my advisory council. I am looking to bring on a few select advisors (5–10) and really hope you can be one of them. This would be a very small time commitment but would make your helping me more official, and with your permission, I would list you on my website as a member.*

*Thanks for considering my request. I'd like to set up a call so I can answer any questions you have and hopefully bring you on board. I'll follow up with you later this week.*

*Best,*
*[Your Name]*

## CHAPTER 5: TURN MOXIE INTO MONEY

Get ready to raise money. Before you raise money, you should meet with advisors, more seasoned entrepreneurs, or coaches who understand the various types of fundraising (angel, venture, loans, crowdfunding, or other) to determine which kind of capital makes the most sense for your business. You may need to meet with several people. Ask an entrepreneur who has raised capital to share his or her story and what some of the greatest hurdles were. These four questions are a great starting point for speaking with advisors:

1. What kind of money should I raise?
2. When is the right time?
3. Where do I learn the fundraising dance?
4. How much equity and control will I have to give up?

Before you meet with your advisors or coaches, fill out this exercise and bring it with you.

1.  Explain what you expect to achieve by raising capital.

> Example:

> I want to distribute my product in stores nationwide (currently just local distribution), but I don't have the capital to produce more inventory and do a national marketing campaign.

a. _____

_____

_____

b. _____

_____

_____

c. _____

_____

_____

2.  What is the "money-making machine" at the heart of your business, and how predictable is it? Include what your challenges are for making this machine work even better.

> Example:

> We sell memberships to our online games for kids, for which our customers pay a monthly fee of $10. We spend about $80,000 per year on marketing, and we currently have 15,000 customers and are making $600,000 in revenues. We grew 30 percent from last year to this year and increased our marketing by only $10,000. We think we can get to 50,000 customers without a big increase in marketing spend. One of our challenges is to find a way to make this money-making machine even better and more predictable so we can double our revenues.

_____

_____

_____

_____

_____

3. What challenges will your business face in becoming scalable?
   Example:
   For each new client, I have to spend about five hours doing the intake and creating a campaign tailored to them. I am the only one in my company who can do that, so if I wanted to bring in five times as many clients I wouldn't have the time to deliver the level of quality service I want. How can I find a more scalable way to deliver my services?

_____

_____

_____

_____

_____

4. Which part of your business is scalable?
   Example:
   If I could find a way to provide low-cost PR services (even if it is only a subset of what we offer) that didn't require as much staff time, I could sell those services online, and it wouldn't require any or many new staff to oversee new clients.

_____

_____

_____

_____

_____

5.  Before you raise venture capital, learn the dance. Go over this list of "dance steps" needed to succeed in raising venture capital with an advisor or coach to see which ones you have down, and where you need help. Give yourself a Readiness score for each one on a scale of 1 to 5, with 1 being *So ready* and 5 being *Far from ready*.

**I present like a pro:**

I know what problem I am solving.      Rating \_\_\_\_\_

Why now? Why me?      Rating \_\_\_\_\_

I credential myself well.      Rating \_\_\_\_\_

I have a confident and authentic presentation style.      Rating \_\_\_\_\_

I can paint a big picture.      Rating \_\_\_\_\_

I know my numbers.      Rating \_\_\_\_\_

I can talk about "the business of the business" and
    my reliable, repeatable revenues.      Rating \_\_\_\_\_

I can explain why my business is scalable.      Rating \_\_\_\_\_

I know the competitors in my space and what
    differentiated my business from theirs.      Rating \_\_\_\_\_

I have a great team.      Rating \_\_\_\_\_

I am coachable.      Rating \_\_\_\_\_

I am conversational in venture capital.      Rating \_\_\_\_\_

I have a good lawyer.      Rating \_\_\_\_\_

I have practiced my pitch with an audience.      Rating \_\_\_\_\_

# CHAPTER 6: SLIP INTO SOMETHING MORE COMFORTABLE

1.  Networking with maximum efficiency. When you consider going to a networking event (conference, summit, cocktail party), start using the quadrant chart system to help you decide if the event will be worth attending and to track the outcome. Ask: Will I find people there who can help me solve short- or long-term problems? Will I meet potential strategic partners? Will it double as a social event that will give me good energy?

2.  Where *won't* you be the smartest person in the room? What are three networks you could join or attend on a regular basis that you are pretty sure will help you go to the next level in your business and where you will not be the smartest person in the room (industry conferences, entrepreneurs organizations, TED Talks, etc.)?

    a.  _____

    b.  _____

    c.  _____

# CHAPTER 7: DELEGATE YOUR WAY TO THE TOP

1.  Find your own Best and Brightest Times (BBT).

    Step 1 (allow 3 days): Track everything you do for three days and how long it takes. At the end of each day, write down everything you did, from the time you spend getting dressed for work to answering emails and going to the supermarket.

    Step 2 (allow 15 minutes): Create a spreadsheet and group the activities into categories like Brain Work, Workout, Play Time with Family/Friends, and Chores. For example:

**Brain Work**
*   Looking over sales figures.
*   Reaching out to mentors and advisors.
*   Writing.
*   Reading business books.

**Play Time**
*   Activities with friends/partner/spouse.
*   Activities with kids.

## Chores

- Shopping for food.
- Shopping for drugstore items.
- Shopping for clothes.
- Paying bills.
- Doing laundry.
- Answering emails.

Step 3 (allow 15 minutes): On a different tab of your spreadsheet, write down when you think you do each type of work best. Compare that to your actual schedule and see if you are truly using your precious hours when you are at your BBT. Then start changing your schedule to honor these times. Make sure to tell people why you are making these changes so you can foster maximum buy-in.

Step 4 (ongoing, about 30 minutes a week): Team up with a friend or fellow entrepreneur who wants to get better at delegating. Check in once a week to see what is working and share best practices.

2. What are three things you can delegate? Outsource three things to a family member or VA that you are doing at home. Put in parentheses the name of the person you will delegate the job to. Do the same for work. Make sure you do the job yourself first at least once so you can hand it off properly. Trust but verify: hand it off and make sure it was done correctly. Give feedback if it wasn't so that it works out better the next time.

## Home

Example:

Put away kids' laundry (babysitter).

Clean the house or apartment (cleaning service).

a. _____

b. _____

c. _____

**Work**

Example:

    Set up my appointments (assistant or VA).

    Organize my digital or physical files (intern).

a. _____

b. _____

c. _____

# CHAPTER 8: PUTTING THE PERSON BACK IN YOUR PERSONAL LIFE

What is your plan for taking care of yourself?

1.   Here are three things I will do to stay healthy and care for myself:

    Example:

    Go running two times a week with my friend Laura.

    Keep the office fridge stocked with healthy snacks.

a. _____

b. _____

c. _____

2.   Here are three things I can do to combat stress:

    Example:

    Take my dog for long walks two to three times a week.

    Go to a yoga class.

a. _____

b. _____

c. _____

# ONLINE RESOURCES

**Access to Capital Tool Kit.** This free resource from the National Women's Business Council has an overview of types of capital, how to access them, and which is right for your business. Go to http://nwbc.gov/sites/default/files/NWB_infographic5_101714_r5%20%282%29.pdf.

**Astia.** A nonprofit with four thousand members around the world, including investors, entrepreneurs, and executives. Astia's programs encourage women's full participation in the start-up ecosystem by providing access to capital, ensuring sustainable high growth, and developing leadership skills. Astia is raising its first fund as of 2015. astia.org

**Belle Capital USA.** Early-stage angel fund in the digital, mobile, Internet (IT), technology-enabled products and services, life sciences, medical devices, health IT (digital health), and clean tech market sectors. bellevc.com

**Golden Seeds.** Angel investor network and venture fund that invests in women-led companies. Since 2005 Golden Seeds has invested over $70 million in more than sixty-five women-led companies. goldenseeds.com

**Juliapimsleur.com.** Resources and online courses to expand on the concepts in *Million Dollar Women*.

**Levo League.** Provides mentors among experienced men and women who want to help younger women professionals and entrepreneurs get ahead. You can ask them questions online, or connect with local Levo mentors and peer groups. levo.com

**National Women's Business Council.** A nonpartisan federal advisory council created to serve as an independent source of advice and counsel to the president, Congress, and the U.S. Small Business Administration on economic issues of importance to women business owners. nwbc.gov

**SBA (Small Business Administration).** A U.S. government agency that provides support to entrepreneurs and small businesses. sba.gov

**SCORE.** With over three hundred locations across America, SCORE has volunteers ready to sit down and discuss any business person's business needs and link them to a local mentor. score.org

**Springboard.** Accelerator program for women based in Washington, D.C., that combines in-person events with strategic connections to women founders. Springboard portfolio companies raised $6.6 billion in financing. sb.co

**Women 2.0.** Hosts conferences and creates content, community, and events for aspiring and current innovators in technology. women2.com

See juliapimsleur.com for an updated list.

# GLOSSARY

**Accelerator.** Short-term programs (usually three months) in which an entrepreneur trades equity for cash, shared resources, and mentoring. Includes educational components and culminates in a public pitch event or demo day, where investors come to learn about the companies and potentially invest.

**Accountability group.** A small group (two to five people) that meets regularly, united around everyone achieving his or her goals, which are shared with the group. Members of the group keep one another on track, or "accountable."

**Advisory board.** Advisors who provide strategic and tactical advice to the management of a corporation, organization, or foundation. The informal nature of an advisory board gives greater flexibility in structure and management compared to a board of directors. Unlike a board of directors, the advisory board does not have authority to vote on corporate matters or bear legal fiduciary responsibilities. Many new or small businesses choose to have advisory boards in order to benefit from the knowledge of others, without the expense or formality of a board of directors.

**Amortize.** The spreading out of capital expenses for intangible assets over a specific period of time (usually over the asset's useful life) for accounting and tax purposes. Amortization is similar to depreciation, which is used for tangible assets, and to depletion, which is used in reference to natural resources.

**Angel investor.** An investor who provides financial backing for start-ups or entrepreneurs using his or her own money. The capital an angel investor provides can be a onetime injection of launch or seed money or ongoing support to help the company get to the next milestone, such as launching a new product or raising a round of new capital.

**Burn rate.** How much your company is spending each month to run the business. Gross burn is actual cash expenses per month. Net burn is revenues per month minus actual cash expenses.

**Close.** Final stage in taking in new investment, when the paperwork has been executed and the funds have been received.

**Conversion rate.** The percentage of users who take a desired action on a website (e.g., sign up for a newsletter or purchase a product or service) versus the number of users who visit the site. If there are 10,000 visitors to your website and 200 buy your product, then the conversion rate is 2 percent.

**Convertible notes.** A legal agreement for short-term debt that converts into equity. In the context of seed financing, the debt typically automatically converts into shares of preferred stock upon the closing of a Series A round of financing. For example, investors loan money to a startup as its first round of funding, and then rather than get their money back with interest, the investors receive shares of preferred stock as part of the startup's initial preferred stock financing, based on the terms of the note.

**Distribution channels.** The chain of businesses or intermediaries through which a good or service passes until it reaches the end consumer. A distribution channel can include wholesalers, retailers, distributors, and the Internet.

**Due diligence.** An investigation of a company in which a person is considering a potential investment. Due diligence serves to confirm market research, material facts, management references, and so on.

**EIN.** Employer identification number. Also known as a federal tax identification number. When it is used to identify a corporation for tax purposes, it is commonly referred to as a tax identification number. It's like a social security number for your business.

**Emotional intelligence.** The ability to monitor one's own and other people's emotions, to discriminate between different emotions and label them appropriately, and to use emotional information to guide thinking and behavior.

**Equity.** A stock or any other security representing an ownership interest.

**Gross margin.** A company's total sales revenue minus its cost of goods sold, divided by the total sales revenue, expressed as a percentage. The gross margin represents the percentage of total sales revenue that the company retains after incurring the direct costs associated with producing the goods and services that it sells. The higher the percentage, the more the company retains on each dollar of sales to service its other costs and obligations. The margin is a company's profit on sales before deducting the cost of goods sold or any other expenses, such as shipping or overhead.

**Hockey-stick growth.** A sharp increase that occurs over a period of time. The line connecting the data points resembles a hockey stick, with the "blade" formed from data points shifting diagonally, and the "shaft" formed from the horizontal data points. Hockey-stick charts have been used as a visual aid to show dramatic shifts.

**Incubator.** Also known as business incubation programs. They typically offer office space, business skills training, and access to financing and professional networks and can last from several months to several years. Incubators typically do not take equity. You must apply for admission.

**Institutional investors.** Operating companies or organizations that pool large sums of money on behalf of others and invest those sums in securities, real property, and other investment assets. Banks, insurance companies, retirement or pension funds, hedge funds, investment advisors, and mutual funds fall into this category. Angel investors are not institutional investors; venture capital firms are. In other words, angel investors invest their own money, VCs invest other people's money (although the partners typically are required to have some skin in the game, amounting to 1 percent+ of the total fund).

**Key performance indicators.** Quantifiable measures that a company or industry uses to gauge or compare performance in terms of meeting its strategic and operational goals. Also referred to as key success indicators.

**Liquidation preference.** A term used in investment contracts to specify which investors get paid first and how much they get paid in the event of a liquidation event such as the sale of the company. It refers to the "preference" that investors (angels and VCs) typically require and gives them a choice upon liquidation to either (a) get their money back or some agreed ratio thereof or (b) convert their preference shares to common and participate pro-rata in the exit that way. Liquidation preference helps protect venture capitalists from losing money by making sure they get their initial investment back before other parties. If the company is sold at a profit, liquidation preference can also help them be first in line to claim part of the profits. Investors (angels or VCs) are usually repaid before holders of common stock and before the company's original owners and employees.

**Margin.** The amount of profit on any given product or service sold. Margins break down further into gross margins, operating margins, and net margins.

**Pitch deck.** A brief presentation, often created using Keynote, Power-Point, or other slide sharing software, to give an overview of your business plan. The pitch deck is used during in-person or online meetings with potential investors and partners.

**Proof of concept.** When a prototype of a product or an approach to a certain business problem is thought to be viable and feasible, such as when customers are paying for it and it is meeting with customer satisfaction.

**Runway.** The amount of time until your start-up runs out of cash, assuming your current income and expenses stay constant. Typically calculated by dividing the current cash position by the current monthly burn rate.

**Scalable.** A business that has the potential to grow very rapidly, usually because it is based on a platform that can be expanded at low incremental cost and with low incremental human input.

**Series A, B, C, D, etc.** This is the legal term for the various rounds of financing of a company. Depending on the needs of the company, a Series A round of financing may be enough to propel the company to the point at which it can stand on its own with its operating cash flow. Successive venture capital rounds are named alphabetically.

**Stock options.** The rights to purchase equity in your company, which you can grant to management or key employees, board members, or advisors. They represent the option, or right, to buy common stock in the future at a preset low price. They can be exercised at that price once they have vested, which is typically after a period of years.

**Strategic partnership.** An alliance between two companies, usually formalized by one or more business contracts, which allows both companies to leverage their assets and/or customer base. It may involve investment or coinvesting in a project or initiative.

**Sunk cost.** A cost that has already been incurred and thus cannot be recovered (i.e., cost of creating a product).

**Term sheet.** A document outlining the material terms and conditions of a business agreement, specifically investment terms. After a term sheet has been executed, it guides legal counsel in the preparation of a proposed final agreement.

**Tranche.** A French word that means "slice" or "portion." In investing, it refers to when a company closes a transaction and receives the funds in two or more increments. Tranche can be used to ensure appropriate timing for the receipt of funds or to allow the company to hit certain necessary milestones before receiving the balance of the funding.

**Unique value proposition.** A statement that summarizes why a consumer should buy a product or service. It should cite reasons that the product will add more value or solve a problem better than a competing product.

**Venture capital.** Money provided by investors to start-up firms and small businesses with perceived long-term growth potential. This is a very important source of funding for start-ups that do not have access to capital markets. It typically entails high risk for the investor, but it has the potential for above-average returns. It is typically invested in the form of equity (e.g., an ownership share).

**Wallet share.** The percentage (share) of a consumer's spendings (wallet) allocated to products in a particular category.

**Working capital.** A measure of both a company's efficiency and its short-term financial health. The working capital ratio (current assets/current liabilities) indicates whether a company has enough short-term assets to cover its short-term debt.

# NOTES

## INTRODUCTION

1. I have changed the names and identifying characteristics of investors.
2. See the glossary for definitions of "gross margins" and all business terms.
3. According to a 2009 report prepared for the National Women's Business Council, from 1997 to 2002 the number of women-owned firms increased at twice the rate of all other firms. Center for Women's Business Research, "The Economic Impact of Women-Owned Businesses in the United States," nwbc.gov/sites/default/files/economic impactstu.pdf, p. 1.
4. When I started writing this book, the number of women with $1 million in revenues was 1.8 percent (Emily Maltby, "Women-Owned Businesses Make Strides," *Wall Street Journal*, March 21, 2012, http://online.wsj.com/articles/SB10001424052702304636404577294292971 667480); now it's grown to 3 percent, still a very small number (per a 2014 National Women's Business Council report).
5. "Women's Money: A New Vision for Women and Money," Women's Money, http://www.womensmoney.org/about-us (retrieved November 24, 2014).

6. Sharon Hardy, "Launching Women Owned Businesses on to a High Growth Trajectory," NWBC.gov, http://www.nwbc.gov/research /launching-women-owned-businesses-high-growth-trajectory (retrieved November 24, 2014).

7. American Express OPEN, *The 2014 State of Women Owned Businesses Report*, March 2014, http://www.womenable.com/content/user files/2014_State_of_Women-owned_Businesses_public.pdf, p. 1.

8. Jessica Canning, Maryam Haque, and Yimeng Wang, "Women at the Wheel: Do Female Executives Drive Startup Success?," Dow Jones, 2012, http://www.dowjones.com/collateral/files/WomenPE_report _final.pdf.

9. "Women who have discontinued businesses were nearly twice as likely as men to cite inadequate financing as the reason they stopped their businesses." Donna J. Kelley, Abdul Ali, Candida Brush, Andrew C. Corbett, Mahdi Majbourhi, Edward G. Rogoff, Babson College, and Baruch College, "GEM USA 2012 Report," Global Entrepreneurship Monitor, 2012, http://www.gemconsortium.org /docs/2825/gem-2012-womens-report. "The leading cause of business failure for women across developing and industrial nations is lack of access to capital." Global Entrepreneurship Monitor 2012 Women's Report, http://www.gemconsortium.org/docs/2825/gem -2012-womens-report.

10. "Women-owned firms started life with only 64 percent of the capital of male-owned firms and were less likely to tap outside financing over their lifetime, including loans, angel investments, and venture capital. Less startup and growth capital means slower growth." Rebecca M. Blank, "Women Owned Businesses in the 21st Century," U.S Department of Commerce Economics and Statistics Administration, October 2010, p. 16, http://www.esa.doc.gov/reports/women-owned -businesses-21st-century.

11. Jeanne Meister, "Job Hopping Is the 'New Normal' for Millennials: Three Ways to Prevent a Human Resource Nightmare," Leadership (blog), *Forbes*, August 14, 2012, http://www.forbes.com/sites /jeannemeister/2012/08/14/job-hopping-is-the-new-normal-for -millennials-three-ways-to-prevent-a-human-resource-nightmare/.

12. Deborah Spar, *Wonder Women*, cited in Nancy M. Carter and Christine Silva, "Opportunity or Setback? High Potential Women and Men During Economic Crisis," Catalyst, 2009.

## CHAPTER 2

1. Brown, *Daring Greatly*, p. 64.
2. "#93: Sara Blakely," in "The World's More Powerful Female Entrepreneurs of 2014," Forbes.com, May 28, 2014.
3. Albert Mehrabian, *Silent Messages: Implicit Communication of Emotions and Attitudes*, 2nd ed. (Belmont, CA: Wadsworth, 1981).
4. Mollicone-Long, *Think or Sink*, p. 33–34.

## CHAPTER 3

1. Brown, *Daring Greatly*, p. 56.
2. Amy Gorin, Suzanne Phelan, Deborah Tate, Nancy Sherwood, Robert Jeffery, and Rena Wing, "Involving Support Partners in Obesity Treatment," *Journal of Consulting and Clinical Psychology*, no. 2 (April 2005): 341–43, www.ncbi.nlm.nih.gov/pubmed/15796642.

## CHAPTER 4

1. "Research by the Center for Women's Business Research showed that the only statistically significant predictor of whether a woman business owner will obtain capital and expand her business is not length of time in business, size of business or industry—it is her goal for growth." Sharon Hadary, "Top Ten Characteristics of Successful Woman Business Owners," *Enterprising Women* Magazine, 2010, http://www.womensleadershipexchange.com/index.php?pagename=resourceinfo&resourcekey=493.
2. Verne Harnish, "How Can We Improve Leadership?", *Corporate Coach Group*, April 7, 2015, https://corporatecoachgroup.com/blog/how-can-we-improve-leadership (retrieved May 12, 2015).
3. Gerber, *The E-Myth Revisited*, p. 38.

4. See http://www.sba.gov/tools/local-assistance/regionaloffices for a map of all the SBA locations throughout the United States.

# CHAPTER 5

1. The SEC under Regulation D defines accredited investors as financially sophisticated and with a reduced need for the protection provided by certain government filings. Accredited investors include individuals, banks, insurance companies, employee benefit plans, and trusts.

2. Hal M. Bundrick, "The Startup Gender Gap: Men Get 6 Times More Funding Than Women," *Main Street*, August 13, 2014, http://www .mainstreet.com/article/startup-gender-gap-men-get-6-times-more -funding-women.

3. Blank, "Women Owned Businesses in the 21st Century."

4. Geri Stengel, "The Real Reason Women Entrepreneurs Aren't Getting Loans," *ForbesWomen*, April 17, 2013, http://www.forbes.com /sites/geristengel/2013/04/17/the-real-reason-women-entrepreneurs -arent-getting-loans/.

5. Jeffrey Sohl, "The Angel Investor Market in 2014: A Market Correction in Deal Size", Center for Venture Research, May 14, 2015, https://paulcollege.unh.edu/sites/paulcollege.unh.edu/files/webform /2014%20Analysis%20Report.pdf.

6. Clare Chachere, "Annual Venture Investment Dollars Rise 7% and Exceed 2012 Totals According to the MoneyTree Report," *PWC*, January 17, 2014, http://www.pwc.com/us/en/press-releases/2014 /annual-venture-investment-dollars.jhtml.

7. Paul Gompers, Anna Kovner, Josh Lerner, and David Scharfstein, "Skill v. Luck in Entrepreneurship and Venture Capital: Evidence from Serial Entrepreneurs," *Harvard Business Study*, July 2006, p. 9.

8. Brian O'Connell, "Angel Investing versus Venture Capital: Part 1," *eMed*, December 2, 2014, http://www.entrepreneurship.org/emed /angel-investing-versus-venture-capital-part-i.aspx.

9. As a reality check on your odds of getting venture capital, the Center for Venture Research shows recent stats of 300,000 active angels in

the United States who invested about $25 billion in 70,000 compa-
nies, versus 548 active VCs who invested $29 billion in 3,400 com-
panies.

10. The total number of female partners in venture capital firms has
dropped from 10 percent in 1999 to 6 percent in 2014. Of the country's 1,562 venture capital firms, only 139 have a female partner. Professors Candida G. Brush, Patricia G. Greene, Lakshmi Balachandra,
and Amy E. Davis, "Women Entrepreneurs 2014: Bridging the Gender Gap in Venture Capital," Arthur M. Blank Center for Entrepreneurship, Babson College, September 2014, http://www.babson.edu
/Academics/centers/blank-center/global-research/diana/Documents
/diana-project-executive-summary-2014.pdf.

11. Nancy Dahlberg, "Study on STEM Entrepreneurship: Are Women
on a Level Playing Field?," *Miami Herald* blog, October 1, 2014,
http://miamiherald.typepad.com/the-starting-gate/entrepreneurship
-research/ (retrieved December 8, 2014).

12. "Q2 2014 Halo Report Angel Group Valuations Continue Three-
Quarter Climb; Q2 Halo Report Reveals Angel Group Round Sizes
Increase by $1 Million for Healthcare Companies; Texas Joins Top
Three Most Active Regions," Angel Resource Institute, December
2, 2014, http://www.angelresourceinstitute.org/en/Research/Halo
-Report/Halo-Report.aspx.

13. Verne, *Scaling Up*, p. 17.

14. Amy Cuddy, "Your Body Language Shapes Who You Are," TED
Talk, October 2012, http://www.ted.com/talks/amy_cuddy_your
_body_language_shapes_who_you_are/transcript?language=en.

15. Professors Brush, Greene, Balachandra, and Davis, "Women Entrepreneurs 2014."

16. A complete list of programs is available at Ryan Mac, "Top Startup
Incubators and Accelerators: Y Combinator Tops with $7.8 Bil-
lion in Value," *Forbes*, April 30, 2012, http://www.forbes.com/sites
/tomiogeron/2012/04/30/top-tech-incubators-as-ranked-by-forbes-y
-combinator-tops-with-7-billion-in-value/.

## CHAPTER 6

1. Herminia Ibarra and Mark Lee Hunter, "How Leaders Create and Use Networks," *Harvard Business Review*, January 2007, https://hbr.org/2007/01/how-leaders-create-and-use-networks.
2. "Get Your Priorities Right! Part Two: The Important vs. Urgent Matrix," olivergearing.com, March 21, 2013, http://olivergearing.com/get-your-priorities-right-part-two-the-important-vs-urgent-matrix/#sthash.5Xxg8huD.dpuf.

## CHAPTER 7

1. Quoted in Brown, *Daring Greatly*, p. 209.

## CHAPTER 8

1. "Personal ecology: To maintain balance, pacing, and efficiency to sustain our energy over a lifetime of activism." Rockwood Leadership Institute, http://rockwoodleadership.org/article.php?list=type&type=31.
2. Claire Cain Miller, "Mounting Evidence of Advantages for Children of Working Mothers," *New York Times*, May 15, 2015.
3. Spar, *Wonder Women*, p. 255.

## CONCLUSION

1. Jack Welch
2. "Annual Venture Capital Investment Tops $48 Billion in 2014, Reaching Highest Level in Over a Decade, According to the MoneyTree Report," National Venture Capital Association, January 16, 2015, http://nvca.org/pressreleases/annual-venture-capital-investment-tops-48-billion-2014-reaching-highest-level-decade-according-moneytree-report.
3. National Women's Business Council, "The Economic Impact of Women-Owned Businesses in the United States," https://www.nwbc.gov/research/economic-impact-women-owned-businesses-united-states.

4. American Express OPEN, "Growing Under the Radar: An Exploration of the Achievements of Million Dollar Women-Owned Firms," January 2013.

5. Professors Brush, Greene, Balachandra, and Davis, "Women Entrepreneurs 2014."

6. Betsy Mikel, "Startup Communities to Challenge the Tech Gender Cap with $1M from Google," *Women 2.0*, March 6, 2014, http://women2.com/2014/03/06/40-startup-communities-challenge-tech-gender-gap-1m-google/.

7. Here is another stat that makes investors pay attention to the females in the room: among start-ups with five or more women, 61 percent were successful and only 39 percent failed. "Women at the Wheel: Do Female Executives Drive Startup Success?," Dow Jones Private Equity & Venture Capital, 2010.

8. Diane von Furstenberg, quoted in "Von Furstenberg on Her Wonder Woman Comic," *Newsweek,* November 12, 2008, http://www.newsweek.com/von-furstenburg-her-wonder-woman-comic-85349.

# BIBLIOGRAPHY

Amoruso, Sophia. *#GirlBoss*. New York: Portfolio Hardcover, 2014.

Bach, David. *Smart Women Finish Rich: 9 Steps to Achieving Financial Security and Funding Your Dreams*. New York: Crown, 2002.

Ben-Shahar, Tal. *Happier: Learn the Secrets to Daily Joy and Lasting Fulfillment*. New York: McGraw-Hill, 2007.

Braun, Adam. *The Promise of a Pencil: How an Ordinary Person Can Create Extraordinary Change*. New York: Scribner, 2014.

Brizendine, Louann. *The Female Brain*. New York: Harmony, 2007.

Brown, Brené. *Daring Greatly: How the Courage to Be Vulnerable Transforms the Way We Live, Love, Parent and Lead*. New York: Gotham, 2012.

Brown, Brené. *The Gifts of Imperfection: Let Go of Who You Think You're Supposed to Be and Embrace Who You Are*. Center City, MN: Hazelden, 2010.

Brzezinski, Mika. *Knowing Your Value: Women, Money and Getting What You're Worth*. New York: Weinstein Books, 2011.

Collins, Jim. *Good to Great: Why Some Companies Make the Leap . . . And Others Don't*. New York: HarperBusiness, 2001.

Doyle, Bruce. *Before You Think Another Thought*. New York: Hampton Roads, 1997.

Dweck, Carol. *Mindset: The New Psychology of Success*. New York: Ballantine Books, 2007.

Eliot, Lise. *Pink Brain, Blue Brain: How Small Differences Grow into*

*Troublesome Gaps—and What We Can Do about It*. Boston: Houghton Mifflin Harcourt, 2009.

Eyre, Richard, and Linda Eyre. *The Entitlement Trap: How to Rescue Your Child with a New Family System of Choosing, Earning and Ownership*. New York: Avery Trade, 2011.

Fotopulos, Dawn. *Accounting for the Numberphobic: A Survival Guide for Small Business Owners*. New York: AMACOM (American Management Association), 2014.

Gerber, Michael. *The E-Myth Revisited: Why Most Small Businesses Don't Work and What to Do about It*. New York: HarperCollins, 1995.

Goleman, Daniel. *Emotional Intelligence: Why It Can Matter More Than IQ*. New York: Bantam, 1995.

Hadary, Sharon, and Laura Henderson. *How Women Lead: 8 Essential Strategies Successful Women Know*. New York: McGraw-Hill, 2013.

Harnish, Verne, and editors of *Fortune*. *The Greatest Business Decisions of All Time: How Apple, Ford, IBM, Zappos, and Others Made Radical Choices That Changed the Course of Business*. New York: Time Home Entertainment, 2012.

Harnish, Verne. *Mastering the Rockefeller Habits: What You Must Do to Increase the Value of Your Growing Firm*. New York: SelectBooks, 2002.

Harnish, Verne. *Scaling Up: How a Few Companies Make It . . . and Why the Rest Don't*. Ashburn, VA: Gazelles, 2014.

Harris, Carla. *Expect to Win: Proven Strategies for Success from a Wall Street Vet*. New York: Penguin Books, 2009.

Harris, Carla. *Strategize to Win: The New Way to Start Out, Step Up, or Start Over in Your Career*. New York: Penguin Books, 2014.

Harris, Dan. *10 Percent Happier: How I Tamed the Voice in My Head, Reduced Stress without Losing My Edge, and Found Self-Help That Actually Works—A True Story*. New York: HarperCollins, 2011.

Hsieh, Tony. *Delivering Happiness: A Path to Profits, Passions, and Purpose*. New York: Business Plus, 2010.

Huffington, Arianna. *Thrive: The Third Metric to Redefining Success and Creating a Life of Well-Being, Wisdom, and Wonder*. New York: Harmony, 2014.

Ibarra, Herminia, and Mark Hunter. "How Leaders Create and Use Networks," *Harvard Business Review*. January 2007.

Jones, Randell W. *The Richest Man in Town: The Twelve Commandments of Wealth*. New York: Business Plus, 2009.

Kawasaki, Guy. *Enchantment: The Art of Changing Hearts, Minds, and Actions*. New York: Portfolio Hardcover, 2011.

Kawasaki, Guy, and Shawn Welch. *Author Publisher Entrepreneur: How to Publish a Book*. Self-published, 2013.

Kay, Katty, and Claire Shipman. *The Confidence Code: The Science and Art of Self-Assurance—What Women Should Know*. New York: HarperBusiness, 2014.

Kidder, David, and Reid Hoffman. *The Startup Playbook: Secrets of the Fastest-Growing Startups from Their Founding Entrepreneurs*. San Francisco: Chronicle Books, 2013.

Laporte, Danielle. *The Desire Map: A Guide to Creating Goals with Soul*. Boulder, CO: Sounds True, 2014.

Lechter, Sharon, and Sandra Burr. *Think and Grow Rich for Women: Using Your Power to Create Success and Significance*. CD. Grand Haven, MI: Brilliance Audio, 2014.

Mehrabian, Albert. *Silent Messages: Implicit Communication of Emotions and Attitudes*, 2nd ed. (Belmont, CA: Wadsworth, 1981).

Meisel, Ari. *Less Doing, More Living: Make Everything in Life Easier*. New York. Tarchar, 2014.

Mollicone-Long, Gina. *The Secret of Successful Failing: Hidden inside Every Failure Is Exactly What You Need to Get What You Want*. Seattle: Pathfinders, 2007.

Mollicone-Long, Gina. *Think or Sink: The One Choice That Changes Everything*. New York: Sterling & Ross, 2010.

Moore, Geoffrey A. *Crossing the Chasm: Marketing and Selling High-Tech Products to Mainstream Customers*. New York: HarperCollins, 2002.

Northrup, Kate. *Money, a Love Story: Untangle Your Financial Woes and Create the Life You Really Want*. Carlsbad, CA: Hay House, 2013.

Palmer, Amanda. *The Art of Asking: How I Learned to Stop Worrying and Let People Help*. New York: Grand Central, 2014.

Peck, M. Scott. *The Road Less Traveled: A New Psychology of Love, Traditional Values and Spiritual Growth*. 25th anniversary edition. New York: Simon & Schuster, 1978.

Pink, Daniel H. *Drive: The Surprising Truth about What Motivates Us*. New York: Riverhead Books, 2009.

Rabiner, Susan. *Thinking Like Your Editor: How to Write Great Serious Nonfiction and Get It Published*. New York: Norton, 2003.

Reynolds, Garr. *Presentation Zen: Simple Ideas on Presentation Design and Delivery*. Berkeley, CA: New Riders, 2011.

Ries, Eric. *The Lean Startup: How Today's Entrepreneurs Use Continuous Innovation to Create Radically Successful Businesses*. New York: Crown, 2011.

Rottenberg, Linda. *Crazy Is a Compliment: The Power of Zigging When Everyone Else Zags*. New York: Penguin Books, 2014.

Rubin, Gretchen. *Better Than Before: Mastering the Habits of Our Everyday Lives*. New York: Crown/Archetype, 2015.

Ryckman, Pamela. *Stiletto Network: Inside the Women's Power Circles That Are Changing the Face of Business*. New York: AMACOM, 2013.

Sandberg, Sheryl. *Lean In: Women, Work, and the Will to Lead*. New York: Knopf, 2013.

Saunders, Vikki. *Think Like a SheEO: Succeeding in the Age of Creators, Makers, and Entrepreneurs*. Toronto: Barlow, 2014.

Slaughter, Anne-Marie, Joan C. Williams, and Rachel Dempsey. *What Works for Women at Work: Four Patterns Working Women Need to Know*. New York: New York University Press, 2014.

Spar, Debora L. *Wonder Women: Sex, Power, and the Quest for Perfection*. New York: Sarah Crichton Books, 2013.

Steele, Claude M. *Whistling Vivaldi: How Stereotypes Affect Us and What We Can Do*. New York: Norton, 2011.

Sutton, Robert I. and Huggy Rao. *Scaling Up Excellence: Getting to More Without Settling for Less*. New York: Doubleday, 2015.

Thiel, Peter. *Zero to One: Notes on Startups, or How to Build the Future*. New York: Crown Business, 2014.

Wadhwa, Vivek, and Farai Chideya. *Innovating Women: The Changing Face of Technology*. New York: Diversion Books, 2014.

# ABOUT THE AUTHOR

JULIA PIMSLEUR is the CEO and Founder of Little Pim, the leading system for introducing young children to a second language. As the daughter of the language-teaching pioneer Paul Pimsleur, she grew up in the language business. Little Pim has won twenty-five awards for its proprietary Entertainment Immersion Method®, and its products sell internationally in nineteen countries. Pimsleur has blogged about entrepreneurship for Forbes.com since 2012, and she has been a speaker at Stanford University, Yale University, NYU Stern Business School, and the Yale School of Management. Pimsleur has been featured on *Today*, *NBC Weekend Today*, and *Fox News*, and her company has been highlighted in *Business Week*, the *Wall Street Journal*, and the *New York Times*. She won the 2013 Smart CEO Brava! Award for women entrepreneurs.

Pimsleur serves on the advisory board of Global Language Project, a nonprofit that brings free foreign-language instruction to children in disadvantaged public schools, and as volunteer chair of the Entrepreneurs' Organization's Accelerator Program for small-business owners. She earned her BA from Yale and MFA from the French National Film School in Paris and attended Harvard's Executive Education Program. Pimsleur speaks French and some Italian and Spanish, and lives in New York City.